W9-BEK-572

AT THE
FEET *of* JESUS

AT THE
FEET *of* JESUS

A SAFE PLACE IN THE DISQUIET *of* LIFE

BRIAN SHIPMAN

BROADMAN
&HOLMAN
PUBLISHERS

NASHVILLE, TENNESSEE

© 2003 by Brian Shipman
All rights reserved
Printed in the United States of America

0-8054-2614-0

Published by Broadman & Holman Publishers
Nashville, Tennessee

Dewey Decimal Classification: 234.2
Subject Heading:
FAITH \ BIBLE. N.T. GOSPELS \ JESUS CHRIST

Unless otherwise noted, all Old Testament Scripture is from the Holy
Bible, New International Version, copyright © 1973, 1978, 1984 by
International Bible Society. Unless otherwise noted, all New Testament
Scripture is from the Holman Christian Standard Bible, © copyright
2000 by Holman Bible Publishers. Used by permission. Also used is *The
Message,* the New Testament in Contemporary English, © 1993 by
Eugene H. Peterson, published by NavPress, Colorado Springs, Colo.

1 2 3 4 5 6 7 8 9 10 07 06 05 04 03

To the family of
RESTORATION COMMUNITY CHURCH

Contents

Contents

Acknowledgments

Thanks to my wife, Jennifer, who now lies sleeping just a few feet away. Had she married someone else, he would be writing this book.

Thanks to my son Ryan, who has transformed my understanding of how God sees and loves his children.

Thanks to Mike and Vanise Hinesly for their faithful friendship.

Thanks to Derrick and Kara Kinney, Jeff and Leann Weertman, Scott and Robin Moreland, Rob and Tasi Hines, Ron and Ann Spikes, and Martin and Laura Zebreski—dear friends from my first church home group who became the unknowing laboratory mice for the experiment that would turn into this book. Their participation, encouragement, and feedback played a pivotal role.

Thanks to Randy Frazee, pastor of Pantego Bible Church in Arlington, Texas, for his ministry to me as pastor during my extended sabbatical.

Thanks to Bob Hartman of Petra for ministering to my soul with his writings and being kind enough to read mine.

Thanks to Shane and Alisa Reed for their friendship and assistance with the Web site.

Acknowledgments

Thanks to Dennis Tollison, Scott Griffith, and the family of Restoration Community Church for allowing me the privilege of working with them in sharing this message.

Thanks to Chris Hutchison of Livingstone for trusting my early writings enough to give them a chance.

Thanks to Sandra and Cris Law, who probably have no idea that the poem they wrote me nearly twenty years ago is now hanging above my desk.

Thanks to Weldon Doherty for his enthusiastic support long before a single book was published.

Thanks to Mark and Kaylene Cox for planting enough seeds that some of them actually sprouted.

Thanks to Michael and Stephanie Weems for date nights and holding me accountable each week.

Thanks to Bob, Cindy, Ryan, Megan, and Logan Henry. I am fortunate enough to live close to them in this life. In the next life this family will be seated far away in places of much greater honor than I.

Thanks most of all to Jesus, who still allows me to fall down at his feet when I can't take it anymore and still picks me up every time.

Introduction

I love to walk barefoot in the grass. When I was younger, I used to come home from school, take off my shoes and socks, tiptoe past my parents—who would have told me to put my shoes back on—and slip quietly out the door until my soles were buried in the lush St. Augustine carpet of my front yard. Each tiny little blade of grass gently massaged my feet in just the right place. It was an instant pick-me-up.

My wife, Jennifer, also enjoys a good foot massage. At the end of her day, she takes off her shoes and socks too. But instead of going outside, she lies down on the couch and plops her feet into my lap. Where I prefer grass, she prefers hands. Where I prefer walking, she prefers relaxing.

I can't blame her. She spends all day running around chasing a toddler, ushering him through childhood. Her feet and the rest of her body are physically drained by the end of the day. If she does not get a good foot massage, she never really recovers. However, if I spend five minutes giving every part of her feet careful attention and the right amount of pressure, she is a new woman entirely.

If you doubt the value of foot care, remember that podiatrists live to make new men and women out of us by paying attention to our feet. They claim that "time wounds all heels." Some podiatrists tell us that our feet are divided into more than sixty areas called "bioactive zones." The right or wrong kind of pressure on each of these zones is thought to have some effect on every part of your body—from your brain to your belly button, from your liver to your lips, and from your knees to your nose. If this is true, perhaps it is why my wife and I like foot massages so much. Our entire bodies benefit from taking time to focus on the feet.

I think it's about time our feet got a little credit. After all, the twins normally get bad press. Think about it. They are last to arrive on the scene at birth. They are rarely considered attractive. When your mouth commits a sin, your foot is asked to pay a hefty price. Noses never have anything good to say about them. In the shower they are so far from your reach you sometimes do not give them proper attention. Most of the time they go completely unnoticed, though they are largely responsible for getting you from the bed to the bathroom, from the car to the career, and from the mall to the movies.

Chances are that as you read these words, you and your feet are in the middle of the rat race. And though once you ran with great speed, you now notice that your feet are beginning to ache. They are tired, slowing down, unsure of which fork in the road to take next. Occasionally they stumble and send you tumbling down. Sometimes they turn on you with a swift kick, leaving your self-worth bruised and bleeding. Where once you experienced the thrill of victory, now you are face-to-face with the agony of de-feet (I couldn't resist). Your entire body, soul, and spirit have begun to ache. You need rest and comfort. You need encouragement, strength, and hope.

This struggle is what some call a crisis of belief. It happens when what you believe and what you experience seem to meet in contradiction. It happens to the best of us, though when it does, we are afraid to admit it. Prayers go unanswered. You suffer pain or loss with no sense of purpose. The dreams that once drove you now seem unattainable. Stress has erased the exuberance you once had for living. What you thought life would be and what it is are separated by a great chasm of doubt and despair. God seems distant or uncaring, and sometimes you wonder if he is really there at all.

When you feel this way, what should you do? Our culture and even many of our churches have conditioned us to believe that we must suppress, or even deny, these honest feelings and plod forward faithfully. God is in control, so suck in your gut and keep marching in rhythm like a good Christian soldier. Paint a smile over the nagging questions in your mind. Ignore the pain and keep walking. Run, in fact. Faster. Farther. Forward—never backward. Failure is not an option.

This line of thinking is nothing more than a derivative of Darwinism. Only the strong survive. Only the best man wins. To evolve into something better, we mistakenly assume that we must weed out all weaknesses using our own strength. Doesn't make much sense, does it?

There is an alternative, but it is countercultural. It goes against the grain. It will not be easy, but it will get you out of your slump. Ready for this? *It's OK to fall down.* It's OK not to have all the answers or know what to do next. It's OK to say how you really feel. It's OK to sit down right where you are, cross your legs and fold your arms, and refuse to go any further. It's OK to spend some time focusing on the feet.

Not *your* feet, though. Not this time. Don't get me wrong. Your feet need massages and podiatrists and the privilege of walking naked in the grass, but these things only bring temporary physical relief. What about the rest of you, the you inside? Where can the deepest part of you go to find what it needs to get back on track? I'm glad you asked. There is a place you can go, a place not as far away as you might think. Allow me to introduce you to another pair of feet.

They are not attractive, mind you. They are familiar with the ache of wearisome walks against the grain. Together they have climbed rugged mountains and waded through murky waters. They have strolled along peaceful lakesides and through soft, grassy fields. They have also found themselves in deep trouble with no visible way out. Their most obvious features are permanent, prominent scars. Once they stumbled and collapsed under the weight of tremendous hardship.

God fell down.

And even though these feet failed him once, you and I are about to discover together that the worn, callused feet of Jesus have a power that draws people to them. Lives are changed at the feet of Jesus. Fears subside. Prayers are not only heard but answered. Doubts die. Forgiveness flows. Peace prevails.

These feet have been in your shoes. They have walked the paths you walk. They understand where you are and where you would like to be. If you let them, they will guide you. They will *change* you. You don't have to keep pretending that everything is OK. Whether your struggles are big or small, God is ready to pick you up and carry you. It's OK to fall down, but where you fall down makes all the difference.

Join me on a journey that does not attempt to sidestep or deny your struggles, your sins, your fears, and your failures but instead provides a solid path right through them and onto the other side. Come and sit at the feet of Jesus. It's sure to put the spring back into your step.

Peace
in a Busy World

CHAPTER ONE

Everybody today seems to be in such a terrible rush,
anxious for greater developments and greater riches and
so on, so that children have very little time for their
parents. Parents have very little time for each other,
and in the home begins the disruption of
peace of the world.

—MOTHER TERESA

They called him the Bee Man. I called him Dad.

For him it was hobby. For me it was horror. I often watched him—normally from around a distant corner—as he walked freely among the beehives in our backyard. Though the insects circled and sometimes even landed on him, he did not stop his meticulous examination of each rack of honeycomb for signs of the coming harvest. His brain envisioned fresh honey on breakfast biscuits. My brain pictured bees dive-bombing my face.

Most of the time my father allowed me to stay my distance, but occasionally he asked for help. "Come and hold this for me, will you?" he would ask. I tried to make him proud. I would hold my breath and put on a brave face and come closer, but he saw through me every time. "They won't hurt you," he said almost absentmindedly. Yeah, right. Then why do they have stingers made to punch holes in my skin and send pain and poison straight to my brain?

He was always right, though. The bees were as indifferent to me as I was afraid of them. In fact, I do not ever remember a time while checking the hives that a single bee actually landed on me. My confidence would grow ever so slightly with each close encounter among the hives.

However, my training did nothing to prepare me for my first experience with a swarm. Every year in the early spring, a frantic phone call would interrupt an otherwise peaceful Saturday afternoon. My father would answer, and the side of the conversation I could not hear probably went something like this. "Hello? Are you the Bee Man? OK, good. I've got a problem. Thousands of bees are just hanging in one big huddle in one of my mimosa trees. Yes, sir? Oh, you mean that's normal? It's called a swarm, you say? OK. Can you get rid of them for me? Great! No charge? When can you come? Great. See you then."

Dad did not charge anything because for him it was a free hive of bees. I always wondered how my father was able to coax a swarm of bees out of a tree and into a white wooden box, so I asked to come along one day and watch.

We drove across town to a modest home where several neighbors had gathered in the front yard, pointing to one of the trees. I saw the swarm immediately. It was about two feet high and nearly a foot thick, shaped roughly like an oversized watermelon. I decided to watch from inside the truck. My dad decided differently. He grabbed his handsaw and assigned me the task of carrying the hive and a large white bedsheet.

When we came to the point directly beneath the swarm, he unfolded the sheet and spread it on the ground. On one end he set the hive, lid closed, with the small bee entrance facing the sheet. He climbed up in the tree with his handsaw and made his way to the limb that supported the colony.

This action signaled to the other spectators and me to move back. *Way back,* I thought. *Who would want to be anywhere near an angry mob of bees? Surely they would attack the nearest living creature for violating the sanctity of their home.* So I stepped back. Everyone else stepped back. My dad, poising himself in the tree, began to saw.

A moment later the limb cracked, already weakened by the weight of the swarm. Quickly my father positioned the saw on the underside of the limb to prevent peeling and *snap,* the limb yielded and the swarm plummeted downward. With a gentle puff the bees landed squarely in the center of the sheet. I expected them to fly away in rage. Instead, as if driven by an unseen hand, they crawled across the sheet and into the hive. In amazement I drew closer to watch. For a moment I forgot just how close I was.

While most of the bees were obediently entering their new home, those who were not present for the change of address were now returning from their pollen hunt. They were confused, and they were all around me. I stood rooted in fear, trying to convince myself that they would ignore me. Most of them did. About five of them did not.

At least three were in my hair, crawling along my scalp and neck. Two somehow made it inside my shirt and begin marching across my back. I wanted to scream, flail, run like the wind—anything to get them off me. My father saw me. He knew what I was thinking. He looked straight at me and gently said, "Be still. Just breathe easy and be still."

I had two choices: follow my instincts or listen to my father. Against every ounce of will in my body, I chose my father's words because I knew that he knew bees. Though it seemed like hours passed, my father talked me through the crisis, and a few moments later the bees were gone. The sigh of relief I breathed is probably still echoing somewhere in the stratosphere.

Looking back on that memorable day, I realize that life as an adult can sometimes be similar to that moment in my childhood. Instead of the buzzing of bees, though, there is the buzzing of busyness. I am swarmed with things to do, people to see, and places to go. No one could argue that my task list isn't filled with noble doings, but those who know me well might suggest that my demeanor has become a little tense. I assume that the only way to deal with the swirling circumstances of my duties is to run and flail, trying desperately to get them off my back and under control. And yet, even as I do, I hear the gentle whisper of my Father saying, "Be still, and know that I am God."

Maybe you have heard this whisper too. As you navigate the white-water rapids in the river of your life—career, chores, church, family, friends, fun, and everything else in between—you sense that something is missing. You have substituted being busy with being happy, and you are beginning to realize that the two are not created equal. You've known it all along, but you have done your best not to think about it.

You have two choices. You can follow your instincts and continue your frantic pace, or you can listen to the voice of your Father. I do not recommend the former because I have been there, and likely you have too. You know what it feels like, and you do not like it any more than I do. So what can we do? The Bible provides us with the recipe for peace in our busy world in the kitchen of a young woman named Martha.

Based on
Luke 10:38–42

She went over her list again to be sure everyone was counted. Let's see, there's Jesus, his twelve followers, her brother

8

Lazarus and her sister Mary, and herself. Sixteen people for dinner. Wiping the sweat from her brow with the hem of her faded apron, Martha meticulously calculated the portions of time and ingredients she would need to create a world-class feast. Only the best would do for Jesus.

The eldest of three children, Martha's life was a masterful tribute to responsibility. She ran a tight ship, and every move she made was a premeditated step toward a predefined goal. She loved making lists, and even more she loved the check marks that completed them.

Today will be my finest hour, *she thought.* The Son of God has come to my house, and I am in charge. *Her motives were pure. Her heart was true. Her mind was determined. Now she would execute the perfect plan.*

Gather the ingredients. Assemble the tools. Slice. Boil. Marinate. Knead. Where's Mary? She promised to help me. No time to waste. The sun is setting. Pick up the pace. Stir. Toss. Don't forget the bread. Where's Mary? Wash. Shred. Arrange. Move faster. Oh, no! Out of that spice? Substitute! Running late. *A smile wilts.* Where's Mary?! This is not turning out as planned. What to do?

Peek into the living room. Look calm, confident. There she is. She is just sitting there! She knows I need her. Try to get her attention. She isn't looking. Retreat. Work harder. Rehearse a scolding. Plot revenge. Pound a fist. Don't cry. I can do this. I will do this. Oh, no! The bread! I can't do this! *An apron falls to the floor. Staccato footsteps approach.*

In the meanwhile, Jesus and his disciples are in the living room, relaxing from the long journey. They are tired, getting hungry. Some of the men are napping. Jesus is talking. Mary is at his feet, listening.

His words! Penetrating. Probing. Provocative. Cutting through culture and custom. They understand. They see. They care. They know me. He knows me. He loves me!

Mary looks up at Jesus, her eyes locked on his. She's lost in this moment. She has forgotten about every care and concern. She has forgotten about dinner.

"Jesus!" Martha calls, straining to calm her voice and her anxiety. "Lord, please excuse me for interrupting, but . . ." Her voice trails as she reaches in vain for tact. "Don't you know—don't you care—that my sister is sitting in here doing nothing while I slave in the kitchen by myself? Make her help me!" She stands nervously and looks down at Mary on the floor, glaring.

"Martha, Martha," Jesus says, his face widening into a soothing smile, "you are worried about how things will turn out and upset about how they already have. So many things weighing you down! Only one thing is necessary right now. Mary has chosen that one thing, and I will not take that away from her."

Two sisters. Many problems. Two choices. One answer.

Martha's side of the story is intriguing because it so closely parallels our own plight. We are busy, too busy. We are worried, upset, laboring hard to put God and the people around us back in orbit to revolve around our me-centered lives. Like Martha, we have unintentionally traded devotion for drudgery.

The disease Martha carried is marked by one primary pathogen: the *if only* complex. "If only Mary would help me. If only God cared about my situation. If only I had started earlier. If only this meal were perfect." She could not help but imagine that if circumstances were different, her life would be better. Acting on this premise, she focused her time and energy to turning the circumstances her way.

Does this sound hauntingly familiar? We grow up in a world that tries to make us believe popularity, pleasure, power, and plenty are the keys to success and happiness. We accept this formula for living and begin the pursuit. We spend our days striving to manipulate the circumstances in our favor so that *then* we can be happy. Only *then* never comes. As soon as we have managed to get one corner of our little world in order, another demands attention. Still we trod on, whispering, *"If only. . . ."*

I battle with the *if only* complex too. To remind me just how futile this line of thinking is, my wife and I have set up an annual tradition. Every year, on the evening of February 2, we have a guest come into our home and share with us his wisdom. His name is Phil Connors. Perhaps you have heard of him. He is the weatherman for channel 9 in Pittsburgh. He tells the story how, against his wishes, he and his producer and a cameraman once headed to Punxatawney, Pennsylvania, to cover the Groundhog Day festivities. If this is starting to sound familiar, perhaps you have had Phil come to your house too. He is also known as Bill Murray, and he can be found in your local video rental store in the movie *Groundhog Day.* Jennifer and I watch it mostly for the laughs but also for the lessons.

Phil hates Punxatawney. He hates Pittsburgh. He hates people. He even hates the groundhog. His life's mission is to serve himself—to move ahead in his career, impress the girls, look down on adoring fans, and otherwise live the basic American dream. Enter the dilemma: Phil can't advance his agenda because he can't advance the clock. After performing his Groundhog Day duties and hoping to go home the next morning, he awakens only to find that it is February 2 *again.* In a time warp where he is an accidental tourist, he must repeat the same day over and over.

Though at first this seems a curse, Phil has hundreds of chances to make just one day turn out right, but he fails every time. At first he stubbornly but optimistically pursues his selfish dreams. Unrewarded, he gradually becomes bitter and then angry that life is not going his way. Try as he might, Phil cannot seem to work the repeating circumstances to his advantage. He slips into desperation and finally despair. Only when he stops trying to seize the day does the endless day finally cease.

Phil helps me remember that I am not in control of my day. Mary and Martha remind me that God is. And God's control, his providence, is not just some idealistic fantasy. It is an everyday reality, a today reality. It is real enough to take care of your family, your fears, and your finances. And it is intrinsic enough to dissolve worry and despair. Is there a catch? Yes. God will not force his providence on your life. You must accept it. You must clearly and consciously choose to "let go and let God."

Let's take a closer look at the symptoms of and the cure for the *if only* complex.

Symptom 1. Accusation

Our good friend Martha storms out of the kitchen on a mission. She is convinced that her problem is someone else's fault. In one sentence she blames both the divine and the human for her troubles. "Lord, don't You care that my sister has left me to serve alone?" (Luke 10:40).

How quickly this verse from the Bible peels away the scanty defense of our own outward pretensions and goes right to the core of our intensely personal battles. "My employer isn't paying me enough money. My children do not appreciate me. My wife should apologize. That no-good waitress owes me a refill. The driver in front of me needs to get out of my way. If only so-and-so would get his act together. God is not listening to my prayers. God doesn't know. God doesn't understand. God doesn't care."

You may have every right to level a valid accusation against someone else—or even God. But your rights are not the issue here. Your peace is the issue. It is natural to think that to be at peace and be happy you must guard and protect your rights, punishing anyone who infringes upon them in any way. But the attempt to gain peace robs you of it. Imagine a cyclist in the Tour de France pausing on the steepest uphill climb to curse the angle. His goal to win the race would be lost while he whined over the obstacles. Martha lost sight of her original goal—to please Jesus with a memorable meal—when she focused more on the food than her honored guest.

Martha's outburst started long before she left the kitchen. We are not privy to the minutes or perhaps hours of thoughts that evolved from curiosity to confusion to anger and finally to open accusation. And even though Martha could have hidden her thoughts, her plight would not have changed. "Holding it in" only masks the deeper problem.

The real problem lies with the list, that mental list of people and the things they have or have not done to your satisfaction. You have held in your frustration with some people on your list. For others small bursts of steam have escaped. And for some you've let volcanic eruptions loose. Whether internal or external, if you are holding grudges and pointing fingers, you cannot move forward on the path to healing until you forgive every person on your list.

Is that really possible? Total forgiveness for everyone who has ever hurt you in any way? Absolutely. I didn't say it is easy, but it is possible. And it is *necessary.*

Humans are most godlike when they forgive. They are most devilish when they accuse. Accusation and forgiveness are the extremes in the war between good and evil, as illustrated in this passage from the Old Testament Book of Zechariah.

Then he showed me Joshua the high priest standing before the angel of the LORD, and Satan standing at his right side to accuse him. The LORD said to Satan, "The LORD rebuke you, Satan! The LORD, who has chosen

Jerusalem, rebuke you! Is not this man a burning stick snatched from the fire?"

Now Joshua was dressed in filthy clothes as he stood before the angel. The angel said to those who were standing before him, "Take off his filthy clothes."

Then he said to Joshua, "See, I have taken away your sin, and I will put rich garments on you."

Zechariah 3:1–4

Satan accuses. God forgives. It's as simple as that. Notice that it's not a matter of right and wrong. Satan was right in his accusations: Joshua was guilty as charged. Still, in the face of Joshua's many crimes—represented by the filthy clothes—God chose to forgive and restore Joshua.

I know it's not easy. Some of the people on your list are truly guilty, perhaps of heinous crimes. But as long as you accuse them, even justifiably, you cannot experience peace. You've got to forgive every one of them from the heart.

Now might be a good time to put this book down and take your list to God. He knows and understands what it means to be hurt by someone else. If anyone has a right to accuse, he does. The people he created misunderstood his visit to this planet. Some rejected his claims. Others called him names. Some spit on him. A close follower sold him out for a few silver coins. Another denied ever knowing him. The religious people of his day, those who should have loved him most, hated him so much they arranged for his torture and execution. And yet, from his cross of agony, he cried, "Father, forgive them" (Luke 23:34).

He forgave you that day too. He knew all of the hurt you would bring him, and still he chose to love you. In accepting his gift of forgiveness, God asks that you in turn forgive those on your list.

When my two-year-old is hurt, he runs to me with arms out-stretched and cries, "I hold Daddy!" And when I pick him up, he holds on tight. I reciprocate with all I've got. What a wonderful picture of the relationship we have with our Father, God, when we experience pain at the hands of someone else.

Give it a try. Take your list, sit down at the feet of Jesus, and hand it over. Tell him honestly about who has hurt you and how it makes you feel, and then let him deal with it.

In the event that God himself is on your list, it's OK to go to him with that problem too. Tell him openly and honestly why you feel the way you do, and be prepared to have your socks knocked off by his loving and caring response.

Symptom 2. Manipulation

If you don't let go of your list soon enough, you could find yourself entering the second stage of the *if only* complex: manipu-lation. Rather than simply blame others for your problems, you now begin to plan strategies to persuade them to modify their behavior to your liking. Notice that Martha's prayer to Jesus doesn't contain a request; it delivers a command. "Tell her to give me a hand" (Luke 10:40). She attempts to manipulate her master by implying he doesn't care unless he fulfills her request immedi-ately. She tries to use guilt to force Mary into compliance by com-plaining that she "has left me to serve alone."

When I was about ten years old, I found a nickel on the ground next to a vending machine. I promptly and proudly displayed my find to my six-year-old sister. She reciprocated by finding a dime nearby and doing a dance. What was I to do? I couldn't be outdone by a mere child, especially a *girl*. So I feigned humility and offered a trade. "Here. You can have the big one. Let me take that little one off your hands." She bought it, and I pocketed my profit. Some brother I was.

AT THE FEET OF JESUS

Manipulation is a deceptively dangerous craft. It can sneak in as innocently as a playful rant over who will do the dishes. It is the primary catalyst of voices raised, truth twisted, and doors slammed. Put any two people in the same room to call on its dark powers against each other, and neither will walk away happy. A prayer aimed at manipulating God loses its power before it leaves the lips of its author.

James, the brother of Jesus, said it best:

> What is the source of the wars and the fights among
> you? Don't they come from the cravings that are at war
> within you? You desire and do not have. You murder
> and covet and cannot obtain. You fight and war. You do
> not have because you do not ask. You ask and don't
> receive because you ask wrongly, so that you may spend
> it on your desires for pleasures.
>
> James 4:1–3

The word *manipulate* has its origins in a Latin term meaning "to fill the hands." As long as you've got your hands full trying to control everyone else, you will never be free to clasp them together and ask the one in control of everything to solve the problem for you. Every temptation to take matters into your own hands is actually an invitation to seek God's intervention. It's your choice, but I think you'll enjoy the outcome of the latter.

Symptom 3. Separation

Jesus was in the living room. Martha was in the kitchen. Her works of service, though intended to honor God, actually kept her away from him.

God is much more concerned with the relationship than he is with the responsibility. Jesus said, "If you love me, you will keep my commandments." He did not say, "If you keep my

16

commandments, it proves that you love me." The love, the relationship, comes first. The commandments, the duties and service, flow naturally from a good relationship with him.

I have a toddler. His name is Ryan. He can count to ten. He sometimes brings me my socks and shoes. He spots airplanes before I do. He says *please* and *thank you*. And yet, as proud as I am of all his accomplishments, my greatest joy is simply to be with him. I would much rather have him in my lap doing nothing than know he is writing the alphabet in three languages across town in a school for baby geniuses.

You are God's greatest joy. He cannot stand to be apart from you for even a moment. He would rather die, and he did, than be separated from you. So don't get caught in the trap of substituting your Christian duties for spending time daily in his presence. A fire that isn't rekindled regularly will burn out. Learn to develop a rhythm in your relationship, a balance between devotion and service. You can't have one without the other.

The Cure—Simplification

Martha was so concerned about her to-do list that she forgot the one reason she originally made the list: to please Jesus. Jesus reminded her gently but firmly that he would be most pleased if she would simply sit at his feet and spend time with him.

That's where we find Mary—sitting, listening, still, quiet. Her choice probably wasn't an easy one because she knew that preparing dinner was the women's job. She knew her sister's style, realizing that at any moment Martha would be calling for help. But she also knew that Jesus was present. Sitting at his feet was an opportunity she refused to pass up.

Making a conscious choice to spend quality time in the presence of God every day is not easy. Your schedule is already packed. But think about the alternative. If you don't choose Mary's peaceful posture, you have already chosen Martha's frenzy. A few moments in the Word and on your knees will refuel you for the entire day. Not only will you be at peace during your time with God, but he will grant you the grace you need to stay at peace when the craziness around you starts all over again.

You've probably heard before the mandate to have a daily devotional or a quiet time, but like many, you struggle to maintain this discipline. You stand torn between the gentle whisper of your God in the sitting room and the maddening song of the sirens in the kitchen. And, deceived by the voices of the urgent and the immediately tangible, too often you choose the latter.

Ultimately we make this difficult decision based on our underlying sense of purpose. Most of us assume our daily and ongoing purpose is "project management," fancy terminology for the juggling act we do, trying to turn our to-dos into ta-das.

We define ourselves by what we do. When we meet someone new, often the first thing we ask after learning a name is, "What do you do?" In other words, we ask for proof of worth based on primary activity, normally an occupation.

The Bible plainly states that your purpose for living is your occupation. Confused? That's OK, I'm playing with words. The word *occupation* has two basic definitions. You're thinking of the first. I'm thinking of the second. In addition to meaning "vocation," *occupation* means "invasion." During World War II, the Germans occupied France. In the history of Middle Eastern conflict, you will often read about the occupied territories.

Your purpose is to let your life be so occupied by Jesus that you start to look and act like him.

> For those He foreknew He also predestined
> to be conformed to the image of His Son.
>
> *Romans 8:29a*

You have no other purpose. Everything that you do, think, and say emanates from this central theme. You are called to be a clone.

But how? How do you let Jesus occupy—invade—your life to this degree? By following Mary's example and taking the time to sit at Jesus' feet and spend time with him. Only in your reflection of Jesus can you become a reflection of him.

Compare your imitation of Jesus to a mountain lake's midnight reflection of a full moon. In order for you clearly to see the image of the moon in the water, three things must be true.

First, the water must have an unobstructed view of the moon. Tree limbs, tall mountains, and artificial edifices can all stand in the way. There's nothing wrong with any of these things, but if they block the rays of light coming from above, then we will not see the moon. Mary sat comfortably at Jesus' feet and focused all of her attention on the Lord so that her eyes and ears could catch the full impact of his words.

When you get alone with God, get *alone* with God. Remove all distractions. Create a place in your home where you can focus clearly on your Lord.

My wife gets up about a half hour before everyone else and sits alone in a dining room we have yet to convert into a dining room. There she opens her Bible and her heart to God. If my son wakes up early, it distracts her. If I come walking by to get some juice, it distracts her. So I respect her needs and steer clear. If I hear Ryan calling for breakfast before she is done, I whisk him into another room for some quiet morning playtime.

On the other hand, I have to wait until everyone else has gone to bed. I'm wired at night, and that's when I try to make myself available to God. If Jennifer or Ryan do not sleep well, it distracts me. If I did not get enough sleep the night before, sleep distracts me. Jennifer and I do our best to guard our time with God carefully. If we don't, no one sees Jesus reflected in our lives. Rather, they see only Brian and Jennifer, probably at their worst.

The second thing that must occur for us to see a reflection of the moon in our mountain lake is that the water must be clean. A muddy lake doesn't reflect light well. A life tainted by things outside of the will of God cannot be godly.

Mary was comfortable in the presence of Jesus. She obviously had nothing to hide. What do you have to hide? What is going on in your life that keeps you from sitting comfortably in the presence of God? Whatever it is, if anything, you can wipe it out instantly by asking God to forgive you.

There's no reason you can't be clean and pure in the eyes of God. If you are already, then you can reflect him even more. If you're not right now, you can be. Just ask. Then you will be able to spend time with and reflect Jesus in your life.

Finally, a perfect reflection can occur only if the water is completely still. Even if the first two requirements are met, any amount of turbulence will distort the lunar likeness.

Mary sat. She didn't move. She didn't want to. She stayed for as long as it took. Even when Martha demanded assistance, Mary didn't budge.

Spend as much time with God as it takes for you to be completely still and take in everything you need to show his reflection. I need at least ten minutes just to settle down and get started. Typically I do this by listening to a favorite worship song or reading a devotion by a favorite author. Jennifer likes to let the morning sunlight stream in the window to get her in the mood.

Whatever you need to do, do it. Develop a daily rhythm of spending time in the presence of God. Once you do, you will start to notice that the busyness around you doesn't seem so important or taxing anymore. You will begin to find peace.

In all of the days I spent with my father around his honeybees, I never once got stung. And though the hectic pace of your life may surround you on all sides, don't forget the words of your Father: "Be still, and know that I am God."

> *Don't worry about anything, but in everything, through prayer and petition with thanksgiving, let your requests be made known to God. And the peace of God, which surpasses every thought, will guard your hearts and your minds in Christ Jesus.*
>
> *Philippians 4:6–7*

Discussion Questions

Complete this sentence as honestly as you can: If only _____, then I would be happy. How much of your life has been spent working toward, or even thinking about, this goal? Do you think you can be at peace without reaching this goal? Why or why not?

Have you silently or publicly placed blame on others for standing in your way of achieving this goal? Who? Why are they to blame? Is God on your list of the accused? Are any of the people on your list really to blame? Even if they are, can you forgive them? Ask God to help you forgive everyone on your list.

Have you manipulated others in any way in your attempts to achieve this goal? How? Have you prayed to God to fulfill this goal for you—in his way and in his time? Are you more likely to manipulate or pray? Which use of your time do you think is more effective? Which leaves you more at peace?

Do you find yourself staying busy for the sake of being busy? Does your busyness take you away from God and the people in your life whom you know are most important? What changes can you make in your life to be less busy and spend more time with God and the people around you?

Faith in the Face of Failure

CHAPTER TWO

If you have made mistakes, even serious mistakes, there is always another chance for you. And supposing you have tried and failed again and again, you may have a fresh start any moment you choose, for this thing we call "failures" is not the falling down, but the staying down.

—MARY PICKFORD

She sprouted early but bloomed late.

In the third grade she stood a full head and shoulders above her classmates. Her nickname was Too Tall Turkey. At such a tender age, she began to develop an extreme awareness and sometimes shame of her appearance.

By the time high school arrived, most of the other girls had caught up to her maturity. But they surpassed her in confidence. She still felt like her looks could never earn her a beau. The guys sensed her lack of confidence and often overlooked her for the other girls, lending further credence to her theory.

High school came and went without a single date. She entered college and hoped a fresh start would change her luck. Her self-esteem was at its lowest point. During college she watched her roommates date and break up. The guys simply did not seem to notice her. Every now and then someone would show a little interest, but he never came close to her standards.

By the time she made it to her junior year, she was one of the most beautiful girls on campus, but she had never really dated anyone. She began to think she would never marry. She felt like a social failure. She prayed for a boyfriend, but nothing ever changed. One evening during her prayer, she thought she heard God tell her to stop looking for a boyfriend and start looking for him. Reluctantly she obliged, telling God that she would be his child even if she never found a man to call her own.

Less than an hour away from her childhood home was a young man. He was about as average as you could get. He loved playing sports, riding his bicycle, and climbing trees. He never gave his appearance much thought, and despite a few rough spots in junior high, he landed in high school mostly intact.

He dated just a few girls, and each of them for long periods of time. In his mind a girlfriend was a potential wife. He wanted a steady relationship, and one day he wanted to be happily married.

During college he began dating a girl that he decided would be his bride. He gave her a ring, and they set a date. But things did not work out as planned. The relationship ended abruptly, and the wedding was canceled.

He graduated from college carrying the pain of his breakup. He started his career and rented a one-bedroom apartment. Living alone was not part of his plan. He desperately wanted a girlfriend. He felt like such a failure after his last relationship that he wasn't sure he could ever date another girl seriously, much less ask her to marry him. He prayed every night that God would send the perfect girl his way. One evening during his prayer, he thought he heard God tell him to stop looking for a girlfriend and start looking for him. He couldn't imagine life without a mate, but he hesitantly agreed. He said, "God, even if you never bring me a girl, I will serve you."

That week the young man went on a college trip to New Braunfels, Texas, with his new church. Only a handful of young people went, but one of them was a pretty girl whom he had been eyeing for some time. He remembered his prayer, though, and refused to take up chase. Instead, he simply planned to enjoy a day of white-water tubing.

But the river was too low that day, and there was no white water. In fact, they couldn't move at all without paddling. So the group floated lazily together in a small huddle. The young man and the object of his affection ended up together by chance, and they spent the day getting to know each other.

By the end of that weekend, the young man and young woman who had just given up on finding someone else found each other. God put them together and gave them to each other. Two years later they said their vows. Eleven years later they are still happily married and raising a son. She is a spectacular housewife and still the prettiest girl in town. He is working north of downtown during the week and trying to write books on the weekend.

Jennifer and I both thought we were failures. And after we had tried everything else and finally given up, God brought us together. We still talk about "the coincidence" of how we both prayed the same reluctant prayer at the same time, only to see that God gave us what we gave up. He turned two failures into a family.

Failures come in a variety of flavors—dating, dieting, careers, hobbies, weekend plans, marriages, churches, peace treaties, retirement plans, parenting, health. These things can all fall apart and leave you trying to make sense of the pieces. Sometimes the sting of failure is so great that it makes you simply want to stop trying.

The analogy at this point is "I am at the end of my rope." The idea is that you have already been climbing downward trying to find solid ground, and now there is no more rope. There is only an empty chasm beneath you, and you don't know if you can hold on much longer. What do you do now?

At the end of her rope is where we find a woman that we'll call Anna. Her failures left her with little other choice than a most daring act.

Anna, like most girls her age, was

Based on Mark 5:21–43

probably looking forward to marriage. She was interested in boys, and they were interested in her. But her dreams for a romantic relationship shattered when the bleeding started.

After one of her regular menstrual cycles, Anna continued to bleed. It was just a trickle, but it would not stop.

A regular flow of blood meant that Anna was ceremonially unclean all the time. To comply with the religious laws, she could never enter a synagogue. She could not marry because she would touch her husband every day and make him unclean. People around Anna would avoid her to avoid being unclean. Many would assume that God was punishing her. Anna's status changed overnight from being a normal young lady to a social and religious outcast.

But Anna was no pushover. She was determined to beat this problem and regain her former standing. She had dreams of marriage and children. No way was she going to let a little trickle of blood hold her back.

She went to a local doctor and explained her situation. He tried a few forms of treatment, but nothing worked. She visited other doctors who tried other known methods of healing, but all of those efforts failed too. With a substantial portion of her savings gone, she pursued alternative medicines and radical remedies. These doctors performed unproven and painful experiments on her. Instead of getting better, she only grew worse. Her flow of blood actually increased.

The days turned into weeks, then months, and finally years. Her former friends were all married and having children. She could not celebrate their happiness with them because she was unclean. Isolation took the place of relationships. She became a recluse, living alone at the edge of town. She occasionally tried other medicines for her malady but always without success. Her money drained; she withdrew even further. People began to forget about poor Anna. Anna almost forgot about her dreams. She had no father, no husband, no man to provide for her. She barely managed to provide for herself.

And then one day Jesus came to town. Anna had heard many stories about Jesus' power to heal. She was a skeptic at first, but now at the end of her rope, she seriously considered that Jesus might be her only chance. Anna may have one day met a former leper who told her about how Jesus healed him. Whatever the case, Anna's faith in Jesus grew. She believed that Jesus was her only hope, but he was always somewhere else—anywhere but her corner of the world—until today.

When Anna heard people shouting that Jesus was in town, she immediately dressed and ran toward town. Already hundreds of people were gathering around Jesus. Most of them just wanted to be able to say that they saw him. Anna wanted to get close enough to touch his clothes. If I can just grab the corner of his cloak, I know that I will be healed, *she thought. Some might say that twelve*

years of failure had driven her mad. Anna knew that she was think-
ing more clearly than ever.

First she tried to approach him from behind, but the crowd was
too thick. Then she tried to intercept him from the front, but another
man got there first. She recognized him as one of the elders in the
synagogue, a man whose job included making sure that Anna never
got inside because of her condition, a man who had a family and a
daughter born the same year Anna's bleeding started. And now this
man who had kept her away from God kept her away from Jesus.
Jesus was following the man to his home to heal his daughter.

Discouraged, she thought about going home. She thought per-
haps God cared more for a synagogue elder's daughter than for a
poor old maid. But with one last try she circled back and decided
to come in from the side. She sneaked up one alley and back down
another. Emerging as the crowd passed, she flung herself to the
ground and began crawling through a forest of legs and feet toward
the center. Amid a hail of angry shouts, she continued to make her
way until she could see Jesus just ahead. She stood on her feet and
adjusted her shroud to make sure no one could see her face. She
squeezed past a few more people and almost made it. She reached
out her arm as far as she could extend it and stretched even farther
with her fingers. Others kept pushing her out of the way, but she
was determined.

Finally she managed to get her hand close enough to grasp his
cloak for a brief second. And when she did, her bleeding stopped.
It was instantaneous. She could feel the difference even before she
let go of his clothes.

Trembling with joy, she turned back and tried to make her way
through the crowd and back home. That's when she heard Jesus
shout.

"Who touched me?" To everyone else in the crowd, it was the
silliest question they had ever heard. People were everywhere,

pushing and shoving and running into one another and into Jesus. And he asked who touched him? It would be like the President stopping his State of the Union address to ask, "Who's looking at me?"

Anna knew that Jesus was talking about her. She froze and looked over her shoulder, hoping he would forget about her and move on. But he didn't. Jesus kept repeating his question and searching the crowd for an answer. Everyone backed away, unsure what Jesus meant. Was he angry at the crowd for pressing in so tightly?

Anna could hide it no longer. She rushed forward and fell on the ground in the now vacant circle around Jesus. With tears in her eyes, she told him and the crowd the whole story of how and why she slipped unnoticed into the crowd and touched the edge of Jesus' cloak and received healing for her bleeding.

Jesus smiled, a tear running down his own cheek now. "My daughter, your faith has made you well. Go in peace. You will never suffer in this way again."

One week later, as prescribed by the law, Anna brought a sacrifice to the priests to signify the end of her unclean period. The following Saturday she attended the synagogue and sat next to a twelve-year old girl whose father ran the place.

Imagine how the story would have changed if Anna had never run after Jesus. We would never have heard her story. She would have remained alone in her small house and eventually died alone. It might be days or weeks before anyone noticed the grass growing tall around her doorway and the mail stacking up outside. Once someone did notice her, the city would probably take her decomposing body to the garbage dump. The end.

Fortunately for Anna her story did not end in failure, but how many other stories do not yet have a happy ending?

The single mother, divorced and working two jobs to support her children, never has time to make friends—much less consider dating. The teenager, stricken with a deadly disease and now living in the hospital, may never have a chance to walk home on his own or play basketball with his friends. The pastor, who unknowingly accepts a congregation in trouble, watches his dreams of success fall apart in a church split. The childless couple, who long for a baby of their own, so far have only had miscarriages. And then there's your story.

You probably have something in your life that you consider a failure similar to Anna's. You've tried everything you know to change the circumstances, but nothing has worked. You've prayed. You've spent time and money. You've talked to the experts in the field, but no one can help you. Now your only choice seems to be giving up and living with this problem for the rest of your life.

Repeated failure causes a condition that we'll call the *invisible leash* syndrome. It happens to people just as it happens to elephants. When a baby elephant is born into captivity in some parts of the world, it gets a leash. One end of the leash is attached to a collar around the elephant's neck. The other is tied to a metal stake driven deep into the ground. At first the baby elephant has dreams of roaming free. He pulls on the leash and tries desperately to escape. But before long he realizes that he cannot go any farther than the length of the leash. And finally he stops trying.

But as the elephant grows, so does his strength. As an adult he is now strong enough to pull the stake out of the ground and be free. But the elephant has a long memory. He sees the stake and feels the collar around his neck. He doesn't think he can do anything about his situation. And he doesn't. He becomes a permanent prisoner.

Like the elephant, you may have failed so many times that you don't realize you can now be free. All you remember is that you have not succeeded in the past, and you assume this means you will never succeed. There is no way out. So you sit down, bitter and depressed, and remain a permanent captive in a prison with no visible walls.

Humans do not fare well in captivity. We sit and stare and finally stew. We wallow in misery. We look for someone to blame. We develop attitudes that we try to hide from some and cannot hide from others.

I know how you feel. I do not write these words as an impartial observer. I want to show you how I began my journey out of the captivity of hopelessness and back toward the open frontier where the elephants roam freely. Let's start with where you are and take small, deliberate steps toward where you want to go.

It's not fair.

No, it's not.

When I was younger and my parents wouldn't let me have my way, I would say, "It's not fair." My father would reply, "Life isn't fair. Get used to it." Unfortunately I have to agree with him. Life is not fair. It is not impartial or equal. When a drunk driver can walk away from a wreck that takes the life of an entire family, life is not fair.

Now that I am an adult, I sometimes go to God when I cannot have what I want and complain that life isn't fair. And he responds in a way much like my father did. He says:

> *In this world you have suffering. But take courage!*
> *I have conquered the world.*
>
> *John 16:33b*

Fortunately God's response is a little different from my childhood version. Instead of "Get used to it," God says, "Take courage! I have conquered the world."

What does this mean? Which is it? Will I have trouble, or will I overcome? Both, actually. You can't have one without the other. You can't overcome something until it causes you trouble.

Anna spent all of her money and twelve years of her life frantically trying to get past this problem. She suffered cruel medical experiments and watched her condition grow worse. She was isolated from friends. She could not go to synagogue and seek God's help. She lived alone and forgotten. But the day that Jesus came to town, she overcame.

If you could sit down with Anna in an interview and ask her only one question, what would it be? I would ask, "Knowing what you know now, if you had the power to go back in time twelve years and start life over without your condition, would you?"

It's a tough question, because if Anna never experienced her trouble, she never would have experienced that transforming day with Jesus.

Offer cold water to someone who has spent all day seated in an air-conditioned office, and he will probably enjoy it. But give a glass to a runner completing a marathon, and she will relish it.

When you go to the movies, what do you expect to see? Happy people in a coffee shop drinking latte and chatting amiably for two hours? Marriages that never have trouble? Schemes that succeed without any opposition? No. You want to see a protagonist with an impossible goal go through character transformation and beat tremendous odds to overcome all the obstacles. That means a good portion of the movie will be nothing but struggle. The meat of the movie will be tribulation, sandwiched between a good opening and a happy ending.

Our lives are also shaped by struggles. But God is faithful and promises us that he has overcome the world, and we can seek him for help. His power can overcome any failure, no matter how bleak the prognosis.

It's impossible.

No, it's not.

It's easy to think that your problem is impossible to solve when you are on the losing side of the victory. Everything you have tried has failed, and by induction that means everything else you might try will also fail. Therefore, solving your problem is impossible.

Anna believed her situation was impossible. So did her doctors. So did her bank account. So did the friends who abandoned her. But the presence of God changed her mind. She didn't even ask Jesus to heal her. She just got as close to him as she could.

That's what happens when the presence of God comes into contact with failure. It changes things. It changes you. It changes your outlook. It changes your mind.

That's what we need changed most—our minds. In an age where everyone is a skeptic and every postulate immediately encounters the words "prove it," we have trouble believing anything we cannot experience with the five senses.

King Solomon, thought by many to be the wisest man who ever lived, wrote these words:

> Trust in the LORD *with all your heart*
> *and lean not on your own understanding;*
> *in all your ways acknowledge him,*
> *and he will make your paths straight.*
> *Proverbs 3:5–6*

The greatest mind of all time says, "Don't depend on what you think." It's not what you do with your brain that counts. It's the one you trust with all your heart.

When I first felt the call into ministry, I was certain God told me to quit my job and move to the Dallas area to attend seminary. My heart said yes, but my brain said, "Show me the money." I thought that if God were really in this, he would provide a financial windfall before I quit my job to help us move and get settled.

So I began trying to make my own paths straight. Jennifer had just graduated from college with an education degree. We had been married for less than a month. We took a long weekend and hand-delivered her resumé to school districts all over the area. I tried in vain to find a part-time job.

I filled out the application for seminary and mailed it. The deadline for registration approached, and still neither of us had a job or even a thought of where we would live. I had failed. There was no way I was ever going to be able to go to seminary. Therefore, I would never become a minister and fulfill God's call. I had failed, and my life would never be what it was intended to be.

And that's when God said, "Just let go. Let me take care of everything. You've done your thing. Let me do mine now."

So I did. Jennifer and I prepared to move. My legs were literally shaking when I gave our landlord thirty days notice that we were moving. By the next day the house was already leased to someone else. I had twenty-nine days left, and I had nowhere to live.

Two weeks later we still had no arrangements to move, but I walked into my boss's office and said, "I'm giving my two-week notice. I'm resigning. I am leaving to attend seminary." My boss was amazed. He asked what I would do for money. I shrugged and said, "I have no idea."

I walked back to my office in a daze. My brain was screaming at me for being so stupid. I felt like my life was a chess game, and I just voluntarily walked into checkmate. Then the phone rang. It was Jennifer. She had just received a call from a school district near the seminary. They wanted to interview her for a first- and a third-grade position. Later that day my boss called me into his office. He said, "If you can work one week longer, then I can guarantee you three month's severance pay."

The minute I let go of my job, it seemed that God was really moving. Later that month Jennifer and I drove up for her interviews. We were so sure God wanted us there that we signed a one-year apartment lease before knowing if either of her interviews would succeed. Both of them did. She had to choose. And she had always wanted to teach first grade.

God's providence is better than our planning. We don't need to plan nearly as much as we need to trust God to provide. And he will because his middle name is "provide." Well, maybe not his middle name, but one of God's names is "the Lord will provide." In fact, this name is given to us in the first book of the Bible. That's no coincidence. God wanted us to know up front that he can and will provide for all of our needs. All we have to do is trust in his name and leave the rest to him.

It can't be that easy.

Yes, it is.

Of all Jesus' healings recorded in the Bible, this one is unique for two reasons. First, the woman never asked Jesus for healing. She took it. You could almost say that she quietly stole it. And second, this woman did not receive her healing when Jesus touched her or spoke to her. Her life was changed when she touched him.

Despite the differences in her case, the results were the same. She was healed. How? Why? Jesus gave her the same answer that he gave everyone else. He said, "Your faith has healed you." Notice that he did not say, "My clothes have healed you." Faith in Jesus alone brought about the change.

Faith. What is faith? Most of the time we think of faith as believing that God can do something. God can do miracles. God can beat anyone at chess. God can heal bodies. God can change the weather. God can intervene in my circumstances and rescue me from trouble.

Believing that God is capable is not faith, though. Take it a step further. Faith is not just believing that God can do something. It's believing that he will. Now stay with me. I am not saying that you can manipulate God into giving you what you want by sheer willpower and mental effort. You cannot name and claim whatever you want. If you could, then the TV preachers who say that you can wouldn't need to ask you for money all of the time. They could simply believe, and cash would appear whenever they wanted. That's not how it works.

But you can believe—you can know—that God will do something when it lies within the boundaries of his will. In other words, God will when God wills. The apostle John understood this concept and shared it with us in one of his letters.

> *This is the confidence we have before Him: whenever we ask anything according to His will, He hears us. And if we know that He hears whatever we ask, we know that we have what we have asked Him for.*
> *1 John 5:14–15*

Startling, isn't it? The Bible says that you can know for sure that you can get whatever you need from God when you approach him for help.

Now at this point your brain is probably challenging you by saying, "Well, that's all well and good. But since I can never really know if something is God's will, then I can never really have faith enough to see a miracle in my life."

This is where most people miss out on seeing God's power displayed in their lives. We assume that we cannot know God's will.

And so we seek God with only half faith. We know that he can, but we are not sure that he will. How do we know if what we seek is really God's will?

Drum roll, please. There is a way you can know the will of God. To help you understand, I'd like to tell you about a friend of mine named Shane.

Shane works alongside me, both during the day at work and on nights and weekends in ministry. He set up the Web site for this book. He heads up the media ministry at our church. He has worked with me on many ministry projects. As you can imagine, we spend a lot of time together. The more I get to know Shane, the more I understand him. And the more I understand him, the more I know what Shane will do and what he won't. For example, I know that tomorrow at lunch if I suggest to Shane that we go to the nearby Mexican restaurant, he will say no. He doesn't care for the place. He really doesn't care for Mexican food at all. So, even though I know that he is capable of eating there, he won't. So I don't ask. However, if I pick up the phone right now and ask Shane to provide free Web hosting for a friend of mine for a couple of months, I know that he will.

Let's test my theory. I'm going to call Shane right now. Stand by. There. Done. He agreed with no questions asked. I knew he would because I know Shane.

You can have the same confidence when you approach God. All you have to do is spend time with him and get to know him. Then you will know what he will and will not do. The faith you need to see miracles does not come from your efforts. You cannot manufacture it by visualizing the answer. You cannot attend a class that teaches you to reach down into the depths of your being to pull it out. Faith does not come from you. It comes from God. It is a gift that comes naturally to you when you get to know God.

Your relationship with God is the key to finding faith in the face of failure. Get to know him. Take your time with him beyond the daily devotional. Include him in all that you do throughout the day. Whisper praise to him while you sit in the classroom or conference hall. Memorize verses or passages from the Bible that you can take with you throughout the day. Share your concerns with him on your commute. Look for him in the sunrise and the sunset. Watch for the ways he works in your life.

And then, when you feel that failure is sweeping over you like a flood, run to him. Reach past the crowd of distractions that keep you from him until you touch the edge of his clothes. Get to know him, and you will know what he will do. Know what he will do, and you can ask with full faith that he will rescue you from your failure.

Discussion Questions

What failures have you faced in life recently? How have they affected your walk with God? Your relationship with your family? Friends? How have they made you act differently than if you had succeeded?

Think of a time in your life when you struggled at or even failed at something, but in the end managed to somehow come out on top. How did you feel when you finally succeeded? Would you have enjoyed the victory as much if you didn't have to struggle to get there?

Rank your faith in God on a scale of 1 to 10 based on this question: Will God provide you with what you need to succeed in this area? What specific reasons keep you from ranking your faith at a 10?

Explain the difference between the following two statements: a) God can provide me with success; b) God will provide me with success. Which statement represents real faith? Does real faith mean you can ask God for anything and get it? Why or why not? How would your life change today if you exercised more faith in God?

I've Prayed and Prayed—Now What?

CHAPTER THREE

That which you persist in doing becomes easier, not that the nature of the thing itself has changed, but the power to do it has increased.

—RALPH WALDO EMERSON

Pray for Rexx Carr.

This hastily handwritten sign hung at eye level on the glass doorway leading to every entrance of the church building. Church members blinked eyes and shook heads, as if somehow this would help them to see something other than this alarming message. What could have happened to Rexx? He's one of our most faithful members.

The news spread rapidly that Rexx, an electrician, was in a work-related accident. He had experienced a severe electrical shock and now remained in intensive care at the hospital. His injuries were monstrous, and his prognosis was grim. Death was a high probability. Amputation of both arms was almost certain.

Many, however, refused to accept this dismal forecast. I prayed to God often that day, always asking that Rexx's life and his limbs be not only spared but also restored to full function. For the next few days, I sought God many times in tears, hoping for the best.

The phone call came. Rexx would live, but he would lose his right arm at the shoulder. His left arm would be taken at the elbow. His face would need reconstructive surgery. His hips would need multiple operations to give him any chance of ever walking again. I hung up in disbelief and slumped back in my chair.

Almost a year later I visited Rexx at the hospital. He was in a wheelchair and going through aggressive physical therapy. He had a prosthetic arm attached to his left elbow, and with muscle movements he had learned to rotate and grasp with the artificial hand. Rexx drove his wheelchair back and forth past the elevator doors in the crowded hallway. "This is how I pace," he said in an amazingly cheerful tone.

I didn't know whether to laugh or cry. Rexx wasn't pacing for himself. He was pacing for his son. The day before, Josh Carr was playing outside with a friend. They were climbing on a rope they had tied between two trees and over a creek. During one of Josh's turns, one of the trees uprooted and tipped over. Josh landed with a thud in the creek, and the tree landed mercilessly on his skull—fracturing it in several places and burying his head in the water. The other boy was not strong enough to move the tree but heroically managed to prop Josh's head out of the water with a branch so he could breathe. Josh's friend ran with all of his might for help. Minutes later an adult called for an ambulance and came to move the tree, gently bringing Josh out of the water until the paramedics arrived.

Now Josh lay in a drug-induced coma, and the prognosis was unclear. He could not breath on his own. The doctors said his condition was "minute to minute." Rexx was "pacing" in the hallway. Friends and family surrounded his wife. I, too, paced the hallway—talking to others and praying to God for a miracle. I remembered the prayers uttered nearly a year ago, and I looked at Rexx. Was my prayer answered then? Were others' prayers answered? Would God hear my prayer for Josh, a prayer that did not include lifelong rehabilitation for Josh? I prayed that Josh would be restored to complete health.

As I write these words, I continue to pray and struggle to believe that God will hear and honor my request. It is a crisis of my own belief in the power of prayer. Seeing Rexx and seeing Josh in the same hospital with such challenges ahead of them sometimes makes me want to give up prayer altogether.

Perhaps you have felt or do feel the same way. What is the point of prayer? Why pray when what you ask for seems to go unanswered? Why does God seem so silent during your time of greatest need? Where is he?

"Where is he?" Jairus asked himself

Based on
Mark 5:21–43

while trying to see past the crowd ahead of him. "He must be nearby. They said he landed by boat here earlier. I've got to find him before its too late!"

Jairus was chief operating officer of the local synagogue. He did his best to keep the building in shape and provide for all of the basic needs for weekly worship. The community respected him for his dedication, and Jairus enjoyed the honor.

Today, though, Jairus was not walking with head held high. He ran wildly down alleys and nearly fell down turning corners as he tried to stay ahead of the crowd and guess where Jesus might be. Finally, one of his guesses paid off. He could see a man up ahead at the front of the crowd, obviously someone of great importance.

Jairus crawled through a sea of arms and legs until he emerged at the epicenter of the commotion and fell fully prostrate before Jesus. "Please!" Jairus cried in a long, mournful wail. "Please come to my house before my daughter dies. I know that if you just lay your hands on her, she will live!"

Jesus did not spurn Jairus's urgency and immediately agreed to go with him. Jairus brought himself back to his feet and turned toward home. "This way!" he shouted. Wading through the mob, he pleaded, "Let us through. It is an emergency!"

They were halfway there, and Jairus was beginning to believe that he just might be able to see his little girl walk again. Just when his hopes began to rise, Jesus stopped. "What, has he changed his mind!? What is he doing? Why isn't he coming with me?"

The crowd looked surprised as Jesus turned back to them, his face filled with curiosity. Jairus could not contain himself and began a short-lived protest when Jesus spoke. "Who touched me?"

"Who touched him?" *Jairus thought.* "Here we stand among a throng of hundreds, and he stops to ask if someone has touched him? My daughter needs your help, Jesus! Please do not delay any longer."

But Jesus did delay. To Jairus it seemed like hours, but it was only a few minutes. Jesus spoke with an elderly woman who had touched him and received healing. Jairus could not hear their words because he could not believe his eyes. As Jesus addressed the woman and the crowd, two of Jairus's friends approached him with sagging heads. They had been back at the house at the prayer vigil for his daughter, and Jairus knew that their coming could only mean one thing. He could not—he would not—believe it. He turned his face from them and looked back at Jesus, who was still ignoring him as he finished his conversation with the woman.

The men arrived and surrounded Jairus. One put his arm on Jairus's shoulder and struggled to speak. One of them wept. "She's gone. She's gone! Leave this teacher alone now, and come back to grieve for your lost daughter." Jairus looked at them incredulously.

His mouth fell open, and his legs buckled. He would have fallen if Jesus had not reached forward and caught him from behind.

Jesus heard the news but disregarded it. "Jairus, do not be afraid of the words you have heard. You believed in me on your way here. Now believe in me on our way back."

Jairus held onto Jesus' hand as he and Jesus followed the men back to his house. Already many people had gathered outside of Jairus's home, some of them sincere and some of them feigning the display of grief. Jairus now knew it was true. His little girl was dead. What could Jesus possibly do now? It's one thing to heal. It's another to bring someone back from the dead. Only God could do that.

Jesus cautioned everyone firmly to stop the ruckus. "She is not dead. She is asleep!" At first they looked at one another in wonder. And then they laughed. Jairus would never forget that sound. His daughter lay dead. His hopes lay only in Jesus, who said she was not dead. And the laughter he heard just didn't belong. He could find no context for the sound, and he placed his hands over his ears and ran into the house to find his wife.

Jesus instructed his companions to disperse the crowd at once, and he went inside the little girl's bedroom with only her parents and three disciples. She lay motionless on the bed, her head and chest already adorned with flowers. Jairus stood with his wife at the foot of the bed, gazing at the precious face that had fallen so ill in recent days. He knelt quietly and held his breath, watching Jesus' every move.

Jesus approached the little girl confidently and sat down by her side. In a near whisper, Jesus spoke. "Little girl. It's time to get up."

For a split second—nothing. Then Jairus watched in awe as his daughter's eyes fluttered and then opened. She sat up in bed, her face pink with health. Jairus couldn't move. He didn't know whether to go to Jesus or his daughter, so he wrapped his arms around them both as he sobbed for joy.

Jairus's experience is an exquisite depiction of the life of a prayer. First, he had to find Jesus, and it was a struggle. Then his initial hopes were dashed. Jesus seemed to take too long to respond to Jairus's request. Jairus was probably confused and impatient during the interval. And if Jesus' delayed reaction was not enough to endure, word came that the request he made had already been denied. His daughter was gone. His prayer was unanswered. It was too late. Precisely at this crux of conscience, Jesus returned his attention to Jairus and said, "Don't give up. Keep on believing."

We expect prayer to be more of a fast-food drive-through experience than an intense and sometimes long journey of seeking God and his power to help us in situations where we cannot help ourselves. Many give up even though the answer lies just around the next bend in the road. Let's take a closer look at Jairus's own journey and discover together how to get around the pitfalls that distract us from a persistent prayer life.

God seems so far away.

Jairus didn't just make up his mind today that Jesus was capable of healing his daughter. He had heard the stories and believed them. He knew Jesus was his only hope, and when he heard the news that Jesus was nearby, he set out on a mission to find him. But it wasn't easy. The crowd was huge. Everyone wanted a piece of Jesus. How would Jairus ever get through?

How will my prayers tonight ever get through the ceiling? I've asked myself that question more than once. I think of my prayer as a message that must go on a long journey—out of my mouth, through the ceiling, into outer space, and into heaven a billion miles away. Once, as I felt my prayers were getting nowhere, God gently reminded me that my words do not have far to travel. Jesus is with me. God lives inside of the Christian. He is with us at all times. He hears our prayers even before we ask them.

Before they call I will answer;
while they are still speaking I will hear.
Isaiah 65:24

And consider this. Even if the best you can do is pray to a God who seems far away right now, even if your only choice is to pray to a God who might not really be listening, you still have chosen the best option. The alternative is that you have no prayer. The alternative is worry.

Imagine if Jairus had chosen to pace by his daughter's bedside and pound the walls with worry instead of seeking Jesus' help. By late that day Jairus would be making funeral arrangements instead of an afternoon snack.

By definition, worry cannot be effective because it is one-sided. Worry is an unborn prayer. Worry wants something to happen but doesn't tell anyone who can help. Worry paces but does not pray. Prayer is markedly different from worry. Prayer also wants something to happen, but by definition it tells the God who can do something about it.

Worry wrings the hands. Prayer folds them. Worry cannot change anything. Prayer changes everything. Worry is the enemy of prayer. When it grips you, it will convince you that God is far away and unconcerned or incapable of helping you.

To fight worry and submit to prayer, I suggest using a technique that you've probably used many times before. Have you ever walked into a crowded room where everyone was talking? At first your ears hear nothing but noise. Then, as you have time to adjust, you begin to single out individual discussions. Your ears have the ability to focus on just one conversation and then switch to another. Which one you focus on is your choice. And which one you finally choose to join is entirely up to you.

The same holds true with worry and prayer. Each competes for your attention, but eventually you will choose one over the other. And you already know which one is going to make a difference.

Every time you sense yourself starting to worry, try praying instead. Don't "worry" about how your prayer will sound— whether it is calm enough or pious enough. Prayers can be desperate too. Jairus was so desperate he threw himself to the ground and pleaded through tears for his daughter's life. The entire Bible, particularly the psalms, is full of desperate prayers. Read the psalms for yourself and see. These prayers serve as examples. They model the ways we can approach God in the midst of our worry.

God may seem distant when the situation seems hopeless, but he is always available.

It's taking too long.

This is the critical stage in prayer where many give up. Not only did Jairus have every reason to give up, but his closest friends even urged him to stop pursuing Jesus after the little girl's condition led to death.

During this difficult period of waiting that spans the painstaking gap between initial prayer and God's answer, we often find ourselves searching for a reason to explain the delay. Most of the time our reasons attempt to assign motives or attributes to God that do not exist. "God must not care, or he would have already acted." "The Lord is angry with me and is punishing me by giving me the opposite of my request." "God is simply too busy with much more important matters than what I need right now."

Jairus could have easily accused Jesus of not caring. After all, Jairus was there first. Had this female intruder waited her turn, and had Jesus ignored her because of the pressing matters at hand, Jesus would have arrived in time to save the little girl's life.

God does care. He has spent his eternal life doing nothing but caring for all of his creation—including you and me. The Bible is clear on this irrefutable fact throughout. Peter, one of Jesus' disciples, stated it concisely and clearly.

> *Casting all your care upon Him, because He cares about you.*
>
> *1 Peter 5:7*

God does care. He cares so much that he has invited you to take every problem you have and bring it to him with full assurance that he will take care of you.

Jairus also could have assumed that his request would not be granted as a punishment for his sin. He may have even sensed poetic justice because the lady who held Jesus' attention for some time was surely no stranger to this synagogue ruler. This woman pled for healing from a twelve-year-long flow of blood from her womb. Such a condition condemned her by biblical law to be unclean, leaving her in permanent exile from the synagogue. If she had ever begged for leniency and exception, Jairus's job would be to follow the law to the letter and deny her the slightest hint of mercy. And now he may have felt he was too harsh and that Jesus was teaching him a lesson by tending to her needs instead of his dying daughter. But we find later that this is simply not the case.

In all of the cases of prayers answered by Jesus in the New Testament, we never find a single instance where Jesus pauses to say, "First repent of your sin, and then I will entertain your request." Perfection is not a prerequisite to genuflection. In fact, it is just the opposite.

Jairus could also have assumed at any time before, during, or after he reached Jesus that the crowd was simply too large and the woman's request too important when compared to his own. But as our story unfolds, Jairus soon realized that Jesus cared enough about his little girl to leave the entire multitude behind in order to tend to her.

Our worth in terms of a percentage of the earth's population seems small when we do the calculations. We are dwarfs in light of the sheer size and number of everything else around us. We pray, and when nothing seems to happen, we can sometimes assume we have little importance in the vastness of creation. Fortunately for us, however, such a deprivation is not possible. Jesus has allotted portions of his Spirit to each of us who trust in him, and so we are never absent from his attentive ears.

Where does this leave us? If none of these reasons can adequately explain the passing of time between our petition and God's response, what are we to assume?

Fortunately, we are not left to wonder why. God has already answered this question. It is found in the Old Testament story of Daniel. In that story, Daniel prayed to God earnestly for three weeks. Every day he presented the same request to God. Daniel's prayers were more than just bedtime appeals. Daniel was fasting and pleading with God all day long.

Finally, an angel appeared to Daniel and brought him an answer to his prayer. But first he explained the reason for the delay. God did not delay in sending the answer, but the answer delayed in coming. This angel left heaven the moment Daniel uttered his first prayer. On his way, however, he encountered resistance for *twenty-one days* (exactly three weeks) from darker forces, Satan's angels.

Locked in spiritual warfare, this messenger fought valiantly until help arrived and he was able to get through to complete his mission. Imagine if Daniel had given up on his prayers after two weeks and six days. I would be one disillusioned angel if I had to turn back after all of that work.

That may sound a little like science fiction, but it's actually spiritual nonfiction. This is the kind of battle that takes place behind the scenes as you pray. God hears and sends his answer to your prayer the moment you ask, but persistent prayer is what keeps the answer coming.

One reason we have lost the tenacity we need to pray is our misunderstanding of basic Scriptures. For example, Matthew 7:7–8 (NIV) reads like this:

> Ask and it will be given to you; seek and you will find; knock and the door will be opened to you. For everyone who asks receives; he who seeks finds; and to him who knocks, the door will be opened.

We tend to look at the verbs *ask, seek,* and *knock* as efforts that require a single act. After all, that's how we typically read them. But this is far from their intended meaning in this passage. Verbs in the Bible often carry connotations that differ from our normal use in everyday conversation. The words Jesus used when he gave us this encouraging message to pray come across better when we read it this way:

> Keep on asking, and it will be given to you.
> Keep on seeking, and you will find it.
> Keep on knocking, and the door will be opened to you.
> Because everyone who keeps on asking receives.
> The one who keeps on seeking finds.

To the one who keeps on knocking, the door will be opened.

Author's translation

Ask, seek, and knock *continuously* because you will find the answer. The message God gives to us here is "Don't give up if I don't open the door at the first tap. I heard you. I'm getting what you need together, and I'm on my way."

It's no use.

Sometimes the problem in front of you seems like something that doesn't warrant prayer. Either it's too big for God to handle or too insignificant for him to care.

My neighbors and I share two small ponds (tanks for you Texans) in the far rear of our properties. I have the unfortunate privilege of owning the earthen dam that separates these two bodies of water. This dam is important because pond A is about eight feet higher than pond B. If the dam gives way, pond A ceases to exist, and half of my neighborhood can no longer fish from their backyard.

Since we moved here two years ago, a pack of beavers has reversed their traditional role and done their best to destroy this dam. In an effort to travel quickly and unseen between ponds, they keep digging tunnels through it. The tunnels erode in heavy rains, the dam weakens, and the water level of pond A drops lower and lower.

My neighbors tried pouring cement into the tunnels. I have tried plugging them with whatever I could find. The situation only grew worse. Every time a major storm came through, the erosion increased. Most of us, including myself, threw up our hands and decided it was no use. The dam would probably give way one day, and an entire ecosystem would be swept away with it.

Last week I walked out to the dam with my son and noticed that one hole had eroded into a death trap. My little boy, or any other small child in the neighborhood, could easily be sucked into swirling waters with one false step. I started to worry about the state of the dam and the dangerous waters. God seemed so far away as I stood there staring into the gaping hole. That's when I realized that I had never prayed about this. I'm not sure if my prayer included actual words, but right then and there I gave up worry and turned this problem over to God because it was bigger and more expensive than I or any of my neighbors could handle.

Just then I looked up and noticed a small bulldozer clearing brush in the backyard of a neighbor some eight houses away. I remember thinking, *Wow. If only that guy would come down here and spend about a half hour. This whole problem could be solved.*

Later, while I was away at work, this same neighbor came by and talked to my wife. He said he had noticed the water level in the pond dropping and realized that the dam needed repairs. He asked if he could bring his bulldozer down and make the necessary adjustments. I didn't have to guess why this was happening. I thanked God and the man. The next morning my neighbor drove his bulldozer through my yard and out to the dam. Thirty minutes later the dam was repaired, the pond level was rising, and the giant hole was gone.

Nothing is too big for God to handle. He is capable—and willing—to assist you in both the big and the small needs of your life.

Now for an update on Josh Carr. My family and my church have been praying for him for six weeks—since the day of his accident. He is no longer in a coma. He is in his home. He is walking and talking. The doctors are amazed at his recovery. So am I.

Some would say prayer has not had any effect on Josh's situation. We know differently. We know that God has honored our request to restore Josh to health and life.

God does answer prayer. He does care. The key, though, is persistent prayer. Prayer was never intended to be a one-time event. Prayer is a journey. It is a road that begins where you are and ends with the answer you are seeking.

If you have ever traveled a great distance by car, you can understand what prayer is like. Each day you will see and experience new things along your way. Sometimes the way is filled with beauty and splendor. Sometimes it may seem flat and uninteresting. Occasionally you may have to stop and ask someone else to point you in the right direction. And when you have driven all you can for one day, you pull over and stop for the night. But each morning you pick up where you left off. And each day brings you that much closer to your destination.

The road of prayer will sometimes seem hard, and you may grow weary of the travel. But keep in mind that you are not the one behind the wheel. Your Father is driving. He is in control, and he will get you to your destination.

As he takes you closer to your destination each day, you will often be tempted to ask, "Are we there yet?" Every child does.

That's when God will turn to you and say exactly what you would say to your own child. "Almost, my son. Almost."

Discussion Questions

Have you ever, or do you now, feel that God has not answered a prayer? What is the prayer? Why do you think you have not yet seen an answer?

How does this unanswered prayer affect your relationship with God? Does God sometimes seem far away? Because God has not yet seemed to answer this prayer, do you find it difficult to pray for other things?

Why do you think it takes time between the moment you pray to God and the moment he provides the answer? How do you normally feel during the interim? Do you find it difficult to wait? Have you ever told yourself during this waiting period that God must not really care or he would have already answered? Does God really care?

Are there any abandoned prayers in your life that you can renew today? How can you improve the quality and quantity of your prayer life?

Finding
Forgiveness

CHAPTER FOUR

The marvels of conviction of sin, forgiveness, and holiness are so interwoven that it is only the forgiven man who is the holy man; he proves he is forgiven by being the opposite to what he was, by God's grace. Repentance always brings a man to this point: I have sinned. The surest sign that God is at work is when a man says that and means it.

—OSWALD CHAMBERS

It was two outs, bottom of the ninth. The bases were loaded. We were one run down. I was the lead man on third base. The pitcher studied his batter, wound up, and released.

It was my first year in the major leagues—of Little League. I was in fifth grade. My team, the Lions, was fiercely determined to beat the green Giants for the pennant. My teammates now looked to me to bring in the tying run. More than anything in the world, I wanted my foot to hit home plate to keep the game alive.

I had more riding on this than just my rookie reputation. On the pitcher's mound stood red-haired, freckle-faced Benny Mitchell—the class bully. His goal in life was to find me on the playground every day and do something—anything—to make me say "uncle." I was terrified of him. Now, after taking a fortunate walk at bat, I had the chance to beat him in front of a crowd of thousands—well, maybe a hundred if you counted our little brothers and sisters playing under the stands.

Benny's partner in crime, Glen Tullous, was the catcher. Glen wasn't out to get me as much as Benny, but he was definitely second in command of recess. I was afraid of him too. As I watched him call the signals for the next pitch, I knew that on a base hit Glen would do all he could to tag me out if the ball came home. Here was my chance to prove myself in front of both bullies. I had to score. I had to. My life depended on it.

In the dugout to my right sat my coach. His eyes were determined—fierce in his passion to win this game. He eyed me warily, knowing that I was not yet one of his proven players. I feared him worst of all, knowing that if I didn't pull this one off I might be spending the rest of the season on the bench.

Back at the pitcher's mound, Benny drew back and threw his pitch. It was low and inside, a ball. Ball two to be exact. I might even get a walk home, but what glory was there in that? Benny's poor show for the evening was no excuse for me to score on a walk. I needed something spectacular, and I needed it now.

Benny waited for the correct signal from Glen, nodded, and wound up. He looked at first base and then at me on third, then back at his man at bat. I squatted low and stretched my right leg forward. My eye was on home plate. Benny drew way back and produced a fastball. It, too, was wild—so wild that Glen missed it entirely. The ball hit the dirt in the batter's box and headed to the farthest reaches of the backstop.

This is it! I thought. *This is my chance. If I score on a wild pitch, Benny will be to blame for the throw. Glen will be shamed for not catching the ball and tagging me out. My coach will praise me for my quick thinking. The crowd will go wild. And I will tie the game and keep us in the running.* My moment for glory had come.

In a flash I darted for home at full speed. I watched the catcher throw off his mask and turn around, searching desperately for the ball. The pitcher instinctively left the mound to cover the plate. Still I ran. I was halfway there. I was going to make it. I looked over and saw that Glen had found the ball. He picked it up. He threw it to Benny.

I'm not going to make it. I'm not close enough. Panicking, I threw on the brakes and slammed into reverse. As I headed back to third and glanced over my shoulder, I saw that the ball had reached Benny and kept right on going. Benny missed the throw! I still had a chance. Though my momentum was headed in the wrong direction, I reversed again and headed for home.

Only a few feet away, I prepared for victory. My pace was too slow for a dramatic slide, but that was OK. I would still be a hero. I looked over at Benny as if to taunt him. That's when I saw that Benny had already managed to turn around, grab the escaping ball, and throw it back to Glen, who was standing firmly in the center of home plate.

At this point everything went into slow motion. Once again I turned around and headed back to third. The third baseman was coming toward me with his glove extended. Glen tossed the ball over my head to him. I was trapped in the "hot box." The pitcher and the third baseman were closing on me, alternating possession of the ball as they moved in for the kill.

Despite all my efforts and gyrations, Glen tagged me out halfway down the baseline. The Giants cheered. Benny grinned. Glen said, "Gotcha."

I looked over at the dugout, now directly in front of me. My coach stood up. He was holding the record book in his hands—a heavy, green, spiral-bound book of pages that held the stats on each player. He didn't look interested in writing anything right now. He lifted the book over his head with both hands, as high as he could reach. His bottom lip was tucked under his teeth in anger. He brought down the book with all of his might and slammed it onto the concrete floor of the dugout.

I can still hear the "thwack" of that book. I can still see the dirt from the dugout floor rushing upward and away to escape the collision. I can still see the look of disappointment in my coach's face, followed shortly by similar expressions from my teammates, my parents, and the rest of the fans. Game over. I blew it. Time to go home. The bullies triumphed, and I let everyone down. No one would ever forgive me. Ever.

My baseball career lasted only one more season. I didn't have much interest in playing after that. My coach didn't have much interest in playing me after that. It took a long time for me to get over that day. I still feel a little guilty sometimes when I think about it. Only the years have managed to ease the pain of that failure.

It hurts, doesn't it? Failure. Especially when you have no one else to blame but yourself. When we do something that we know is wrong, something happens inside. Our conscience relentlessly points the finger of guilt, and we must do something to alleviate the resulting cognitive dissonance (a fancy two-word phrase that means your brain is uncomfortable and needs to do something to alleviate the tension).

I'll let you in on a little secret: everyone is a failure. Everyone. You. Me. That nice little old lady down the street. The Bible says plainly that every person who has ever lived, except Jesus, is guilty of sin. *Sin*. A word that you and I have heard many times before, but I think its meaning still needs clarification. The popular definition of *sin* is "evil" or "moral wrong." Surprise—that's not what it means. To *sin* literally means to "miss the bull's-eye." If you are out at the firing range testing your rifle and you fire ten shots at thetarget, you are "sinning" if you do not hit it dead center every time.

When you see the word *sin* in the Bible, it means to fail to live up to God's purpose for your life. Stealing from your neighbor is not a sin because it is inherently evil; it is a sin because God has better plans for you than thievery and better plans for your neighbor than being robbed.

When you fail to live up to God's purpose for your life, you are guilty of sin. You and I don't want to hear it, but we are guilty. Sin is a crime. And, as you and I know, crime demands punishment.

Now we have painted ourselves into a corner. I'm a sinner. You're a sinner. Punishment is inevitable. But I don't *want* to be punished, so I must find a way to avoid paying the price for my crimes. I must escape.

Two primary (dare I say favorite) methods of securing escape from the guilt of sin and its required punishment come to mind.

Fight

In high school debate class they teach you that you can argue either side of any issue effectively; simply know your topic and know your audience. I have sometimes adapted this technique to justify my own misbehavior. For example, I know that if I am home and my son needs a diaper change, it is my turn to change it. That's the deal because Jennifer has changed them all day. But I don't *want* to change the diaper. I *hate* changing diapers, so my opening arguments begin.

"Ladies and gentleman of the jury. The state of laziness will in this case prove to you beyond a reasonable doubt that my client has worked eight long hours today, not to mention the two hours battling heavy traffic, and is therefore exempt from any domestic duties—namely the posterior of his posterity. Thank you."

Jennifer is rarely impressed or persuaded by my oratory. Likewise, your friends, family, coworkers, and other associates have little time for excuses—valid or not. No one wants to hear why you didn't, can't, or won't do what is right.

One of the hardest things to do when you are wrong is admit it, because if you admit you are wrong, your bank of self-worth becomes overdrawn. There is a negative balance. Someone must pay to make things right, and you certainly don't want to pay. So, instead of admitting you are wrong, you fight in order to justify yourself.

That need for justification is hardwired into your conscience by God, but you will never get it by fighting for it. In fact, just the opposite is true. Justification and forgiveness come only when you openly admit your faults to God.

> *If we say, "We have no sin," we are deceiving ourselves, and the truth is not in us. If we confess our sins, He [God] is faithful and righteous to forgive us our sins and to cleanse us from all unrighteousness.*
>
> *1 John 1:8–9*

Frightening, isn't it? Going to the God whose mark you have just royally missed and saying, "You know that plan you had for my life? I tossed that idea out the window and did what felt good to me at the time. Maybe next time." Fortunately, though, our God is a forgiving God. Though there are and will be consequences to your sin, God will not require you to serve the sentence for your crimes. You see, in the Bible there is only one acceptable punishment for the crime of sin—the death penalty. But God loves you so much that he came to earth and paid that price for you so that when you trust him and admit to him that you have failed, you will be given the gift of a clear conscience and eternal life with God.

So don't fight. Make it right. Admit your sins to God. He promises to wipe the slate clean and get you going in the right direction again.

Flight

If fighting is too messy for you, or if your sin hasn't become exposed enough to require such tactics, you can always retreat. Cover your tracks. Hide the addiction. Reach into your bag of masks and pull out whichever one is appropriate for the moment.

Millions of people have hidden addictions and habits that are not part of God's purpose for their lives—from the dramatic sins of alcoholism, adulterous relationships, drugs, and pornography, to the overly excused sins of anger, lust, envy, pride, impatience, self-centeredness, gluttony (ouch!), and so forth.

You can't hide the "smaller" sins behind the "bigger" ones. All it takes is one sin to make you guilty. You can't hide any sins, big or small. God sees all and knows all. You and he both know the truth about your life and how you live it.

Remember the story of the first sin? Adam and Eve ate a piece of fruit. How could that possibly be a sin? Remember, sin is not a societal evil. Sin is something outside of God's purpose. Everything they had was part of God's purpose, except for one little tree. And even though God said clearly not to touch it, Adam and Eve were stubborn. They chose to visit the tree, stare at the fruit, entertain a serpentine sales pitch, pluck it from the branches, and consume it. Later that same day, in the cool of the evening, God walked through the garden, hoping to spend time with his children. But he could not find them. They were hiding. Ironically, they hid among all the other trees. They tried to cover their wrong by submersing themselves in right, a tactic not unfamiliar to you and me. Adam and Eve did not want to see God or go anywhere near him because they knew that their sin would be exposed.

God knew where they were before he asked. He knew what they had done before he heard their confession. He knew that his penalty of death could not be reversed.

So God acted. First, he instituted the consequences: man must work hard and toil away while woman must subject herself to her husband and experience pain during childbirth. And both of them were banned forever from the garden of Eden.

Second, for the first time in recorded history, God took life. God killed. But he didn't take the lives of Adam and Eve. He took the lives of innocent animals to make clothing from the skins, clothing that would serve as a temporary covering for Adam and Eve's shame and a permanent reminder of their failure. The death penalty was satisfied by an innocent sacrifice that foreshadowed the coming of Jesus.

God knows your hiding places. He knows what you have done and are still doing. He really wants to walk with you and talk with you in the cool of the day, but your secret sins have caused you to run and hide, denying him the privilege. Rather than kill you, he has taken the life of his one and only Son to serve as a permanent covering for you. His death on the cross provides forgiveness once and for all.

Don't hide from God. Don't deny your sins. Take them to God and accept his merciful response of forgiveness.

Neither *fight* nor *flight* confronts the truth of your sin nor eases the pain of your guilt, but you and I both know we often depend on them to get us through the day. Using either of these methods to escape the consequences of our sin is like getting caught in the hot box trying to steal home on a wild pitch. And guess what? You won't make it. You're out. Game over. All of heaven is watching, and your conscience is slamming your record book down like a judge's gavel. You blew it.

In practical terms, how do we really come to grips with our own shortcomings and make them right? Come with me to a little dinner party, and I'll show you.

Based on
Luke 7:36–50

Meet Simon, a prominent member of the community. He prefers flight to fight in his struggle against guilt. He hides it beneath layers of pious robes and religious symbols attached to his wrists and forehead. He cloaks it with a mouth readily spouting memorized Bible verses. He whitewashes it by trying to convince himself that others are much worse than he is. If someone dares question his integrity, he points to his title of "Pharisee." He crouches behind the letter of the law, but in so doing he misses the spirit entirely. He is our host for the evening.

In the same town, on the other side of the tracks, is a woman. We don't even know her name. She, too, has a guilty conscience. The Bible is deliberately vague on the nature of her sin. Though many guess she was a prostitute, her particular problem is unknown. Perhaps her critics attempt to assign her a sin with which they do not struggle, just so they can disassociate themselves. Not so fast. This woman represents anyone and everyone.

She is so consumed by guilt that she would trade her most valuable possession for relief. And that's exactly what she does. Hearing that Jesus is nearby, she seizes a jar of perfume meant for some other special occasion and runs to Simon's house.

Imagine this woman, breathless and pale from haste, standing in front of Simon's house. It's almost comical, considering the strikes she has against her. As a woman, she has no cultural privileges to invade an all-male dinner party. She has no religious title or affiliation. Her perfuming plans pose no precedent. Her sins are known all over town, including here. With all composure lost, she rushes forward, tears streaming down her desperate face.

Inside the house Simon is seated smugly, knowing that the most popular man in the country is now seated at his table. He feels important. He feels proud. He's already planning to outwit Jesus with a brilliant theological discussion when a commotion erupts in the back.

Two worlds collide as the woman manages to get past the servants and invade the dining room. Simon is appalled. An uninvited guest now ruins his perfect evening. He knows this woman. He knows this woman's story. To Simon, a holy God and a sinful human have no right to be in the same room together. He wants her out.

Jesus knows this woman and her story, too, but his reaction is noticeably different. He recognizes the anguish on her face and the tears in her eyes. They are formed in the fountain of regret. He does not look away or move aside when she stands over him, shoulders slumped and knees bent. To Jesus, a holy God and a sinful human in the same room present an opportunity for reconciliation. Jesus doesn't even flinch when the unpredictable unfolds.

Tears. Hair. Kisses. Perfume. All applied liberally. This woman does not merely fall down at the feet of Jesus. She bathes them in all she has. She knows that Jesus is the only one bigger than her guilt, and in response to his forgiveness she expresses her love.

Ironically, as the sinful woman celebrates her forgiveness, Simon's need for and resistance to it is exposed. You can see this in how he has treated Jesus. As host of the dinner, Simon overlooked three basic but important customs for prominent guests. He did not greet Jesus at the door with the traditional kiss on the cheek. He did not pour oil on Jesus' head—a cooling, comforting, and respectful courtesy. And he failed to have a servant wash Jesus' feet from their dusty travels.

Simon does not celebrate Jesus because he does not recognize Jesus as the author of forgiveness. Simon is in flight, pointing the finger at others to distract attention from his own faults. He judges the woman for her sin and Jesus for not recoiling from it.

Two people, desperate for clear consciences and freedom from the stranglehold of sin, each meet Jesus simultaneously but on different terms. One of them leaves dinner a new person. The other leaves with a guilty heart still beating under layers of religion.

What do you do with your sin? Do you fight? Are you in flight? Would you like to find forgiveness for your sin and freedom from your guilt? You can. But you can't do it by hiding or avoiding what you have done. If you're going to clean out the closet, you don't paint the door. You open it and take everything out.

Identify

The first step in finding forgiveness is to identify the areas of your life where you have missed God's mark.

Simon the Pharisee could not identify any sin in his life. His sin was hidden beneath layers of self-righteousness, pious robes, and an attitude of "I am never wrong." And because of this, he did not find forgiveness. However, the sin of the woman who anointed Jesus' feet was not unknown. Jesus knew her sin. Simon knew it. And above all, she knew it. She came to Jesus just as she was. To find forgiveness we must do the same.

Sometimes my family and I go out to eat for dinner. We sit down around a table and talk and eat and have fun. My son provides most of the entertainment. He is still learning to use a fork. Sometimes he gives up and uses his hands to pick up what he wants to eat. By the time the meal is over, my son's face and hands are comically covered with multicolored stains. I take a napkin and dab it in water and wipe his face and hands to make him presentable.

After we finish eating and go home, I sometimes give Ryan a bath. When I get him under the bright lights of our bathroom and get his clothes off, I notice food stains that I did not see earlier. The face and hands that I thought were clean under the dim lights of the restaurant now prove to be far from it. I will sometimes find food particles on his neck and chest, where they had been hidden by his shirt.

I cannot identify the areas where Ryan needs special cleaning until I can see him clearly. He does not take a bath in his clothes or in the dark. Everything comes off, and all the lights go on.

That's how God wants you when he gives you a bath in the soothing waters of forgiveness. He wants to see everything. He wants to know everything. And then he wants to clean everything.

Sometimes we do not even know that we need forgiveness until we come before God. And even if you recognize a few of the obvious areas of your life where you are not living right, you will not see everything until you stand before God. God is light, and his light will reveal much more than you can see by yourself.

Isaiah was a great Old Testament prophet. He was a great man of God. But one day he came closer to God than he ever had before. And that encounter helped him realize that he needed forgiveness.

> *In the year that King Uzziah died, I saw the Lord seated on a throne, high and exalted, and the train of his robe filled the temple. Above him were seraphs, each with six wings: With two wings they covered their faces, with two they covered their feet, and with two they were flying. And they were calling to one another:*
>
> > *"Holy, holy, holy is the LORD Almighty;*
> > *the whole earth is full of his glory."*
>
> *At the sound of their voices the doorposts and thresholds shook and the temple was filled with smoke.*

*"Woe to me!" I cried. "I am ruined! For I am a man
of unclean lips, and I live among a people of unclean
lips, and my eyes have seen the King, the* LORD
Almighty."

*Then one of the seraphs flew to me with a live coal
in his hand, which he had taken with tongs from the
altar. With it he touched my mouth and said, "See, this
has touched your lips; your guilt is taken away and your
sin atoned for."*

Isaiah 6:1–7

Notice the progression of Isaiah's character. First, Isaiah saw
the Lord for who he is, a holy God. Then, Isaiah became acutely
aware of his own sin. He saw the great distance between who God
is and who he was. His immediate response was to identify a particular offense that he had not noticed before. Isaiah realized that
he was a man whose mouth needed a good washing with God's
soap. And that's exactly what he got.

God already knows the particulars of your sin, but he wants
you to know them too. He wants you to identify your sins individually so that he can forgive them individually.

Many times I hear, and sometimes I am tempted to say, a
prayer like this: "God, forgive me for all of my sin." That is a
great prayer indeed, but it is only the introduction to what must
be a deeper and more meaningful entreaty that asks forgiveness
for each sin separately.

It's a painful thing to identify your own sin. The woman who
came to Simon's house wept real tears before Jesus announced her
forgiveness. Isaiah cried, "Woe to me!" before the angel touched his
lips. We, too, can and ought to be horrified by what we see in our
own lives. But do not lose heart. The sorrow we feel for what we
have done is only the first step in eliminating its source permanently.

Confess

It's one thing to know where you have fallen short, but it's another to admit it to someone else.

The woman in our story does not audibly confess her sin. She didn't have to. She confessed her sins silently to Jesus because they were between her and Jesus alone. In addition, let's examine her posture and her actions more closely. They give us a picture of how we should confess our sin to Jesus.

At least three courtesies were normally expected of the host of a dinner party in the first century. Simon offered none of them. She offered all of them. In them we see a poetic illustration of her confession.

A good host of any dinner party would provide household servants to wash the feet of his guests from the day's dusty travels. Simon did no such thing, but his uninvited guest did just that—with her own tears and her own hair. In so doing she acknowledged that Jesus was and would continue to be her honored guest. She confessed before the other guests and before the world that she was renouncing her former way of living and allowing Jesus to replace the sin in her life.

When you confess a particular sin, you are openly admitting that what you did was wrong. And, by inference, you commit to avoiding the same mistake in the future. You are choosing a new path. You are choosing to live God's way instead of your own. You are allowing Jesus to replace the sin in your life.

Another courtesy that Simon overlooked was kissing Jesus on the cheek when he arrived. Such a custom signaled to the guest and any witnesses that he was welcome in this house. The woman did not kiss Jesus on the cheek, but she did kiss his feet—over and over again.

Have you ever kissed anyone's feet? I have, but, believe me, the list is short. And the criteria for earning such a privilege are high in my book. In yours, too, most likely. Only my wife and child have ever received such a courtesy from me, and until God blesses me with more children, they will presumably remain the only ones. They are the people I love the most.

Confession helps us to see just how much God loves us. Confession is available to us for one reason, the love of God. He demonstrated that love for us by dying on a cross and providing the right for us to confess our sin and find forgiveness. And his love for us makes us realize just how much we love him.

The kisses of the sinful woman were her demonstration of love for Jesus. You, too, will experience the truest love for God when you find forgiveness at his feet.

Back at our dinner party, we notice one final practice that Simon overlooked. Simon did not anoint Jesus' head with oil. Beyond the refreshing qualities of this custom, an anointing with oil can also signify the beginning of a kingship. King David began his reign with an anointing from the prophet Samuel.

The woman anointed Jesus with perfumed oil that filled the whole house with its fragrance. Her actions announced to everyone that Jesus was now the king of her life.

When a new king takes over a kingdom, the rules change. When you confess a sin to God and ask for his forgiveness, you willingly submit yourself to God as the new king of that difficult area in your life. Forgiveness does not wipe the slate clean so that you can get it dirty again. Your confession cleanses you from the past sin and prepares your defenses against future sin in the same category.

Confession implies repentance. To repent is not to feel sorry. To repent is to turn from the sin you confess and walk in a new way, God's way. As the new king of your life, he will give you the power to do just that.

Accept

Once you have identified and confessed the individual sins in your life, God forgives you. You are clean. The bath is over.

When Jesus forgave the woman who anointed him, he said, "Go in peace." She could now return to her home and her new life with the calm assurance that her guilt was gone.

Sometimes, though, we miss this last part. "Go in peace." Though forgiven, our regret lingers. The sorrow that brought us to repentance fails to go away. The memory of what we have done seems more powerful than the knowledge that God has forgiven us.

I remember vividly feeling this way one Sunday morning at church. I sat in my pew as the service started and stared blankly ahead. We were about to witness a baptism. The pastor was standing in the water with a new Christian, ready to submerse her as a sign of her new and forgiven life with Jesus.

And while she stood forgiven, I felt haunted by the sins of my past. My whole life suddenly seemed to be nothing but failure to live up to God's expectations. I longed to go back to the beginning like this young lady and experience God's forgiveness for the first time. Even though I had already confessed and received forgiveness for all of them, they still haunted me.

I glanced hopelessly heavenward and noticed something in the ceiling—a long, narrow slot. This opening was the pathway for a hidden screen that could be raised and lowered as needed for multimedia presentations in the service. It made me think about the day I would stand before Jesus and be judged for all of my deeds. I could picture myself standing there while a giant screen played back my sinful life for all to see. I sighed and started to look back down when I noticed something else.

Just as the pastor baptized the young lady, the movement of the waters cast an eerie reflection on the ceiling in the exact location of the opening. A spectacular display of lights danced all around it.

And then I remembered something else: the church had never installed the screen. There was no screen.

God immediately spoke to my heart through this unexpected little parable. There is no screen to display the sins of my past because I have already asked God to forgive me. Both the brand-new Christian in the waters and I stood before God with the same level of forgiveness. I didn't have to go back to the beginning to find release from my guilt. I just had to accept the forgiveness that God had already granted.

When you ask God to forgive you for a specific sin, you do not have to ask again. If you do ask again, God isn't going to forgive you again. He's going to remind you that he has forgiven you already.

You and I both know, though, that sometimes this is easier said than done. Human nature makes it difficult for us to accept God's forgiveness. There are two specific cases where we have tried to place limits on God's limitless grace.

First, we seem to believe that there is a limit to the number of times we can ask forgiveness for the same thing. We get caught in a sinful habit, and we find ourselves every day pleading for mercy. Eventually we are even afraid to ask for forgiveness because surely God can no longer tolerate this repetitive behavior.

Obviously God wants you to break your sinful habits, but he is not going to deny you forgiveness today because you have already filled his quota. God does not keep count.

The disciple Peter once thought there must be a limit on forgiveness, so he asked Jesus about it.

> *Then Peter came to Jesus and asked, "Lord, how many times shall I forgive my brother when he sins against me? Up to seven times?"*

> *Jesus answered, "I tell you, not seven times, but seventy-seven times."*
>
> *Matthew 18:21–22 NIV*

Jesus was not establishing a hard limit. He was playing with numbers and telling Peter that whatever limit he thought there might be, he should multiply it and make it bigger because there is no limit. If there is no limit to the number of times we are to forgive those who hurt us, you can be sure that God has no limits on how often we can receive the same from him.

The second case where we sometimes have trouble believing that God can forgive us pertains to the individual sin itself. Instead of asking, "How many?" we ask, "How big?"

Does God forgive the really "big sins" like murder, rape, child molestation, and worse? What about the biggest sin you have committed? Will God ever forgive you for that?

> *I tell you, people will be forgiven every sin and blasphemy, but the blasphemy against the Spirit will not be forgiven.*
>
> *Matthew 12:31*

God forgives all sin, no matter how big, except for one. And as you hold your breath in fear that you might be guilty of it, relax. You're not capable of perpetrating such a crime if you are a Christian. The only known instance of it occurred two thousand years ago when a group of unbelievers publicly, falsely, and maliciously called the Holy Spirit "Satan" when Jesus performed a miracle. Their disbelief and hatred toward the love and work of God persisted to such a degree that they willingly forfeited their opportunity ever to trust in Jesus.

But as the first half of this verse emphasizes, every other sin imaginable is eligible for God's grace and forgiveness. Nothing you do can ever erase that opportunity.

When you ask God to forgive you, he does—always and without hesitation.

Whatever the reason for your delay in accepting God's gift of forgiveness, now is the time to lay down the burden of your shortcomings. Jesus has already killed the beast of guilt on a hill called Calvary. All you have to do is bury the body.

Asking God's forgiveness seems almost too easy. It is and it isn't. Let's give it a try, and you'll know what I mean.

If you are not alone already, find a quiet place where you can be. Take a piece of paper and a pen with you. Sit down. Get comfortable. This may take awhile. However, I assure you that when you are done, you will be a new person.

Read the following verse. It was written as a prayer, so you can recite it as a prayer to God. Do it more than once if that's what it takes to get you to mean it.

> *Search me, O God, and know my heart;*
> *test me and know my anxious thoughts.*
> *See if there is any offensive way in me,*
> *and lead me in the way everlasting.*
> *Psalm 139:23–24*

Let God begin to show you the offenses in you that still require forgiveness. As they come to mind, write each one down on a separate line.

Make your list as comprehensive as memory allows. Don't leave anything out. You may find that some of your sins are so secret and so private that you can't bring yourself to write them down. That's OK. At least write down a symbol or an abbreviation that will communicate to you what you mean.

Once you are sure you have finished, look over your list. Read it from top to bottom. Put a star next to the sins you feel you are most likely to repeat later, the habits with which you struggle the most.

Almost done. Now comes the good part. Grab some tissue because you may need it. Go over each sin, one by one, and ask God to forgive you for it. Here is an example to get you started. "Lord, I was impatient with my wife today. I didn't consider her feelings, and I raised my voice when I shouldn't have. Please forgive me. Help me in the future to treat her with the respect that she deserves. And give me the strength to apologize to her." When you finish with one, move on to the next. Continue this process until you have asked God to forgive you for every item on your list.

When you are done, take the paper and destroy it. God has already annihilated his copy. Now it's your turn. Tear it into shreds and throw it away. Burn it if you have to, but please do so safely.

There. You have identified and confessed your sin. Now you can accept God's forgiveness. It's over. Feel better? You should. You *will*. Now that the deadweight of guilt has been lifted from your shoulders, and your soul, you may find that life is a whole lot sweeter.

Discussion Questions

What is the true definition of sin? In what ways have you missed the bull's-eye of God's plan for your life in recent days? How do you typically defend or justify your sin? Are you more likely to fight or take flight? How have you recently used your favorite method of defense?

What sins exist in your life right now that you have not yet confessed—admitted openly and honestly—to God? What keeps you from confessing your sins to God? Is there any reason not to stop right now and do so?

Do you find it difficult to believe that God can forgive you for anything and everything you have ever done wrong? Why can God forgive you for all of your sin?

Is there anyone in your life you have not forgiven? Can you take the time to forgive them now?

Keeping Your Dreams Alive

CHAPTER FIVE

I learned this, at least, by my experiment, that if one advances confidently in the direction of his dreams, and endeavors to live the life which he has imagined, he will meet with success in uncommon hours.

—HENRY DAVID THOREAU

Why did I do it? Because it was there.

Every summer my family traveled from our home in rural South Texas to the mountains of New Mexico for a two-week sojourn in Red River, New Mexico. Though a ski resort in the winter, Red River was a camper's paradise in warmer months. Our favorite spot was just north of town in an area known as Elephant Rock. There my parents parked our travel trailer next to a swift mountain stream teeming with rainbow trout that didn't stand a chance against my father.

Our campground was called Elephant Rock because far above, at the highest point of a looming pine-covered mountain range, sat a rock in the unmistakable shape of an elephant. For ten years during my summer stays here, I observed this mighty landmark from a considerable distance, wondering what it would be like to conquer the great beast and stand atop her, beating my chest with a victorious pride.

Now, at age sixteen, I was determined to turn my vision into reality. After a hearty breakfast of eggs, bacon, and homemade biscuits, I bid my parents farewell and walked firmly to the edge of camp. I stood still. I stood alone, deep in thought on the winding road that served as boundary between the place I had always been and the place I always wanted to be. From my vantage point it seemed as if Elephant Rock dared me to approach. I took a deep breath and accepted the challenge.

Once I took my first steps on this new mountain, I noticed I could no longer see my destination. From this angle of ascent, Elephant Rock hid shyly behind a crowded company of conifers. The soft sounds of the campground stream began to fade. The climb seemed steeper than I anticipated. Sometimes my path was lined with a soft carpet of decaying pine needles. At other times a wall of jagged rocks forced me to stop and rethink my route.

After roughly an hour or so, I rested with my back against a friendly tree, facing upward and breathing eagerly. The sweet smell of pine lingered in the playful breeze. A restful calm lay over the mountain and me. I couldn't wait to go on.

As I stood to resume my trek, I became abruptly aware of how quiet it was. It was almost *too* quiet. I couldn't hear a sound other than the occasional crunch of my tennis shoes on a stray pinecone. I should have been grateful for the solitude, but instead I realized that I was probably more alone that I had ever been before in my life. Not a soul on earth knew where I was. I'm not even sure I knew where I was. Fear began to set in. What if I got lost? What if a hungry bear discovered me? What if I slipped and fell and no one could hear my cries for help?

I thought about turning back. I rationalized that scaling this mountain wasn't really that important. I continued my climb but at a slower pace. Doubt dominated my debate. I almost changed my mind and headed back to camp when I noticed a ridge up ahead. I reasoned that I could at least make it that far.

A few minutes later I stood on the promontory and peered up ahead. I couldn't see a thing. No Elephant Rock. No mountaintop. Looking down below, I couldn't make out my camp. No road. No sign of civilization. Nothing. My once clear vision now lay shrouded in fog. What was I to do?

After a bout of hesitation, I decided to go onward and upward. My first step after that half-time pause produced an unexpected second wind. I was more determined than ever to make it to the top.

And I did. Two hours later I made it. To the top. I could see for miles in all directions. I could see my camp. I could see a hundred other mountains and valleys all around me. I could see miles of wide-open sky. I could see everything except Elephant Rock.

I thought my adventure was through. It never occurred to me that once I reached the top I would still have further to go. Was it to the right or left? I tested a short distance in both directions and finally decided to head left. I stumbled onto a dirt road and followed it for some time. Finally, I rounded a sharp bend and watched the road circle around on itself. This was it. There was nowhere else to go. Now what?

I then noticed a small white, wooden sign. It stood barely four feet high against a backdrop of towering trees and thick undergrowth. The black, hand-painted letters announced simply, "Elephant Rock." Was this a joke? I could see no path anywhere behind or near the sign. I paced back and forth, looking for other clues. Nothing. With no other noticeable options, I plunged into the forest in the direction that seemed best—right behind the sign.

It was slow going, but with nothing else to go on, I continued. Then, like someone digging for buried treasure, I suddenly hit something solid. Rock. A big rock. It was nearly invisible in the thicket, but it was definitely there. I leaned forward to use my hands and began climbing. Before long my head rose above first one tree and then another. My heart began to pound. I scrambled faster. Higher. And soon, you guessed it, I stood at the highest point of Elephant Rock.

Exhilaration is perhaps the only word that comes even close to describing how I felt at that moment. I jumped up and down. I beat my chest. I held my arms up with my fists clenched, yelling and cheering.

I know it doesn't compare to Everest, but for me it was a life-changing event. There's nothing like taking a vision and turning it into reality.

Somewhere between the vision and realizing it, though, you will inevitably hit "the wall." Marathon runners describe that moment as an extraordinary fatigue that begs the body to stop short of the finish line. Only the strongest wills survive the wall.

Perhaps you are experiencing the wall right now. You have a dream, and you long to go from here to there. But after trying for some time, instead of dancing on Elephant Rock, you're sitting at rock bottom.

The disciple Peter would understand just how you feel. He sank so low once it nearly killed him.

♣ ♣ ♣

Based on
Matthew 14:13–33;
Mark 6:31–52

It was unusually dark on the lake that night. Southward winds cancelled out the northward rowing of twelve strong men. Backs ached. Hands blistered. Arms grew weary. For more than eight hours they had struggled to make a trip that in good winds would have taken less than one. Now, at three in the morning, Peter began to interrogate himself.

Why am I following this man? He tells me to get into this boat and go one way. The wind and the waves tell me to go the other. He tells me he will never leave me, but right now I do not

82

know where he is. He tells me he is the light, but now all I see is blackness.

Stop it, Peter. You know better. You know he is the One. Think about what happened earlier today. I watched him search for a peaceful, shoreline hillside to mourn for his cousin's death, only to find thousands of people ignorant of his grief and begging for his attention. We could have kept sailing, but I heard him say, "No. Look at them. How could I leave them here? They are like sheep without a shepherd. Dock and let me go to them."

He taught them. He encouraged them. He healed them. And when evening came and everyone was hungry, he didn't ask them to leave. He fed them. He had them sit down in groups on the green grass beside the quiet waters—just as I've seen shepherds arrange their sheep, now that I think about it. I watched him take five biscuits and two small fish and bless them into a feast for five thousand men and twice as many women and children. I carried a basketful of leftovers so full that it spilled over the sides.

Still, that was then. What about now? If Jesus is God, why would he send me on an errand he knew I couldn't complete? How could he not know what we are going through? Doesn't he know? Doesn't he care? At this rate I will never reach the other side.

Only later did I realize that Jesus did know. He did care. He could see us all along from atop his prayerful perch. And he knew what he was doing when he sent us into the night. He was preparing us all for a moment we would never forget.

We were all taking another break and debating whether we should just go back to shore for some rest. We argued and laughed. Mostly, we whined. I remember that Thomas had just said he thought the boat might be leaking when it happened.

Nathanael screamed and pointed astern and into the dimly lit night. At first I saw only a wave cresting on its journey inland. Then, as it fell, I saw the unmistakable silhouette of a man walking on the water. He was about ten feet from the boat and simply strolling along, moving faster than the boat. I froze in terror. It was a ghost. I shook my head and rubbed my eyes, figuring my exhaustion was playing tricks on my eyes. But everyone else saw the same thing I did.

As the figure passed by, I tightened my grip on the heavy, wooden oar and wondered if it would serve as a defense against an immaterial spirit. That's when he spoke.

"Don't be scared, guys! It's me. Jesus!"

"It really is Jesus. He's walking on the water." I was so enthralled by this sight that I did what my friends say I do far too often; I opened my big mouth. "Jesus, if that's really you, let me come out there and join you on the water."

Jesus stopped and responded simply, "Come on."

Trembling but ecstatic, I dropped my oar and hurdled over the boat's edge. My eyes were locked on Jesus as my feet landed on solid, uh, water. I was standing! Jesus smiled and stretched out his hand for me to approach. I felt like I was learning to walk for the first time. I staggered but continued, away from the boat and out toward Jesus. Only a few more feet to go.

Just then a swell broke between Jesus and me. I became aware of the spray in my face and the ferocity of the wind. I looked down. My feet were in the water. I was standing in the middle of a giant lake in the middle of the night. I tried to take another step, but I didn't know where to put my foot. In my mouth was probably the best place, though I figured it was a little late.

In that instant my firm footing faltered. I started sinking like I was in quicksand. I panicked. The water rose to my neck. I screamed, "Lord, rescue me!"

In a flash, I saw his feet. They were still standing there in the water, with nothing I could see holding them up. Then I felt his strong hand grasp mine as he pulled me up.

I could tell he was disappointed. He said, "Peter, you little-faith, why did you doubt? You almost made it. If only you had kept your eyes on me."

We climbed back into the boat and sat down. Everyone stared at Jesus and at me. For a moment there was only silence. Then, worship. We all lowered our eyes and stared at the feet that defied nature, and we worshiped him. Truly God was walking among us.

A few moments later it was silent again. Even the wind and the waves were at peace. We could see the shore just ahead. We rowed in silence, taking it all in. I looked back over the lake at the first signs of morning twilight. Then, as we pulled in to shore, Jesus said something that really made me think.

Cut. Before Jesus and the disciples disembark, I have a question for you. Have you ever been in that boat? You thought it would be smooth, sunny sailing to the shoreline of your dreams, but now you're not sure you'll ever see the water's edge. The circumstances are against you. It's dark. Your mind and body are exhausted from working long hours, and you're still getting nowhere.

What may make things even more difficult for you is that you actually thought God was on board with your plans. You thought he was OK with this, maybe even that he actually *told* you to go this way. But now his thumbs-up is fading from your memory. You can't see him or his thumbs. You wonder if he cares or even if he *knows* what you're going through. You question the direction your life is going. You begin to doubt that you will ever realize your dreams.

You are not alone in your feelings. Many others are in the same boat. Some call this experience the "death of your vision." Others say, "It's always darkest before dawn." Everyone—you, me,

Jesus—goes through this valley. What we do when we're at the bottom will ultimately determine if and when we come out on top. Here are a few tips that I picked up from Peter and the other disciples.

Who owns your vision?

The answer to this question will reveal much more than you realize about you, your goals, and whether the twain shall ever meet. When Peter and his friends faced a mountain full of hungry people at the end of a long day, their goal was to get them out of the way. Wish them well, of course, but send them away as soon as possible. Keep in mind that even Jesus earlier tried to lead them into respite and not a rally. The disciples weren't being selfish. They were being *realistic*. The disciples even brought their plan to Jesus. "Here's what we want. How about it?" Sounds reasonable, right? Sure does. But here is where the road forks. The disciples want one thing. Jesus wants another. It's not that Jesus doesn't care about what his disciples want—and need. He just knows that the crowd's needs are more important right now.

Sometimes what you want and what God wants is not the same thing. Notice I said *sometimes*. In just a few hours, Peter wants to walk on water. In that case, Jesus says, "Go for it." So, before we get started with what it means for Jesus to be the owner and author of your vision, don't assume that you must give up your dreams and sacrifice them on the altar of nothing-can-ever-be-fun-anymore. When you have an idea about what you want to do with your life or your day, don't be afraid to pray about it. God may answer, "Great, let's do it!" Or he may say, "Hey, I've got an even better idea."

Either way, the first step in pursuing your passions is to take them to Jesus and see what he thinks. Sounds simple, doesn't it? But you and I are often guilty of not laying our blueprints before God before we start pouring the foundation.

I can think of two examples in my life that illustrate the importance of laying your future at the feet of Jesus. In one I chose wisely. In the other I chose poorly. I'll start out at the bottom and work my way up.

When I saw it, I had to have it. It was maroon and black. It was sleek. It was fast. It had a 5.0-liter engine. It was a 1989 Mustang LX convertible. I saw the ad in the paper, and I drove immediately to the dealer. The car was parked right in the front as if waiting for my arrival.

I should have said a prayer, but instead, the only thing that came out of my mouth was drool. I was afraid to ask God if I could have this because, well honestly, what if he said no? Then I would have to keep driving that ratty old four-door sedan. And how would I ever attract the attention of the future Mrs. Shipman with that old thing?

In a blur I purchased my first new car. I borrowed way too much money and drove it way too fast. In less than two years, the speedometer broke, the convertible top retractor stopped working, I wrecked it twice, and I met the future Mrs. Shipman without the aid of the car. In fact, she thought it tousled her hair. I finally sold it for half of what I paid for it.

The point? God may well have wanted me to have that car, but I did not seek his counsel. I did not invite him into my decision-making process. He did not own my vision of taming the wild horse. So he respectfully withdrew himself from that part of my life, and I rode alone. I didn't enjoy that car like I thought I would because God wasn't in it.

OK, that's a bad example. Here's a better one. In the fall of 1983, I was playing basketball in a church league. We played one game each week at a church gym seven miles away. Every Saturday morning my team would load up in a van and drive to the game. Halfway between my church and the game, we passed a medium security prison. Inside were a thousand violent criminal offenders. The average age of the inmates was nineteen. I was seventeen.

I had passed this prison many times before, but this basketball season I began to look at it differently. I used to think of it as a place to hold evil people. Now, as a brand-new Christian, I felt drawn to this place and the people inside. Each Saturday as we passed, I somehow saw past the razor-wire fence and steel-barred windows. I saw people who needed to hear the good news about Jesus.

On one of those Saturday morning trips, when the feeling hit me the hardest, I remember shaking my head and thinking, *This is crazy! I don't know anything about prisons, and I have no idea how to get inside to talk to these people.* I told God right then that if this crazy idea was part of his plan for my life, he would have to do two things. First, he would have to show me in the Bible that this was something he wanted me to do. Second, he would have to get me inside—behind guards, fences, walls, and bars.

A tall order, don't you think? Not too tall for God. A few months later I opened the Bible and found this verse staring me in the face:

> *The Spirit of the Sovereign LORD is on me,*
> *because the LORD has anointed me*
> *to preach good news to the poor.*
> *He has sent me to bind up the brokenhearted,*
> *to proclaim freedom for the captives*
> *and release from darkness for the prisoners.*
> *Isaiah 61:1*

Some may argue that I took this verse out of context in applying it so directly to my situation, but I can tell you emphatically that God spoke clearly to me that morning. I knew that God wanted me to go inside that prison and reach out to the inmates there. But how?

Several days later I met a man. To make conversation I casually asked what he did for a living. He mentioned his occupation, but then his face lit up as he described his involvement with a weekly Bible study at the prison. He said, "We just lost one of our Bible study leaders, and we're looking for someone to take his place. You wouldn't happen to be interested in joining us, would you?"

My jaw dropped to the floor, to say the least. I had told few people about my interest in prison ministry. But a week later I sat inside the chapel of a medium security prison and shared my faith with murderers, thieves, and rapists. I felt like Peter walking on the water. God owned that vision, and he carried it through flawlessly without any help at all from me. That's what can happen when you give God your plans and you let him own your life.

OK. Enough about me. What about you? You have a list of things that you are doing or would like to do. Have you taken your to-do list to Jesus yet? Is he the sole author and owner of your best-laid plans?

I know what you are thinking. You're afraid God won't like your idea about succeeding in your business. You think he's going to tell you to sell all of your possessions, give all your money to the poor, and go to Africa to become a missionary.

And you know what? He just might. That could be his perfect plan for your life. And if it is, you won't be happy until you do it. However, God also calls people to be successful financial planners, lawyers, doctors, teachers, clerks, and full-time parents. He needs successful people in those positions in order to reach others in their spheres of influence who do not yet know him. So do not be afraid to go to God with your plans for success. And whether he accepts, modifies, or completely rewrites what you had in mind, you'll love the outcome.

This is a critical first step, and most people do not make it this far. Let me emphasize this point plainly. You cannot, and will not, succeed (using God's definition of success) unless you first seek him and what he has in store for you. You will instead spend your life trying to walk on water using only the known laws of physics, which without trickery simply isn't possible.

Once you've actually prayed about God's plans for your life, or even just your day, you should let God continue to own your vision by waiting for his response. Just because you have asked for direction doesn't give you permission to go forward immediately. When Jesus said to the disciples that day, "You feed this crowd," they did not call the caterer. They waited—perhaps because of faith or perhaps because they were simply paralyzed by shock—for Jesus' explicit instructions on what to do next. His instructions were simple. "Go and see how much food we have here." Searching the crowd, they found one small boy with a sack lunch, five biscuits and two fish.

That's all the disciples had to do. They didn't have to plan a banquet, arrange seating, make name tags, or provide entertainment. Their assignment was easy: "Bring me what you have, and I will take care of the rest."

In the same way, when Peter requested to join Jesus on the waves, Jesus said simply, "Come." Peter didn't have to use his brain to calculate gravitational equations or his hands to tie on a safety harness or his feet to strap on water skis. He followed Jesus' simple instructions: "Come to me right now just as you are. I will take care of the rest."

When God does respond to your prayer for direction, not only will he tell you what to do, but he will also save the hard part for himself. All he asks of you is what you have. He will handle whatever obstacles stand in your way because he owns the vision.

What obstacles block your way?

And there will be obstacles. You can count on it. They are there not to block your way but to remind you that you cannot possibly be the one to complete the task at hand. Only God can get you through. Pretend that you are one of the disciples back there on that sunny hillside by the lake. You're tired, cranky. You want peace and quiet. You ask Jesus to send these people home for dinner. Jesus looks you dead in the eye and says, "You feed them. I want you to have them all sit down, and I want you to serve them dinner—right now."

You would do the same thing they did. You would look up and see nothing but a sea of obstacles. *Timing*—it's late and will be dark soon. *Money*—it would take eight months' salary to buy enough food for everyone. *Motivation*—we don't *want* to deal with these people right now. *Location*—this place is out in the middle of nowhere. *Resources*—all we have is a small boy's lunch.

Two thousand years have not changed the most common excuses that we have for not pursuing the call of God on our lives. Time. Money. "Feeling like it." Perhaps instead of looking at these things as obstacles, we have an alternative. What if God has deliberately created an earth bound by hours and economies and frail human bodies so that we would realize up front how powerless we are in our own strength? While most of the world tries to organize and harness these things into rungs on the ladder of earthly success, God has quietly called his children to stop trying to climb their way to the top and instead wait on him to lift them to the heights.

The Old Testament prophet Habakkuk once said it this way:

> *Though the fig tree does not bud*
> *and there are no grapes on the vines,*
> *though the olive crop fails*
> *and the fields produce no food,*

though there are no sheep in the pen
and no cattle in the stalls,
yet I will rejoice in the LORD,
I will be joyful in God my Savior.
The Sovereign LORD is my strength;
he makes my feet like the feet of a deer,
he enables me to go on the heights.

Habakkuk 3:17–19

Favorable circumstances and practice are not the keys to success. Jesus did not expect the disciples to become masters of calendar and checkbook in order to have compassion on this crowd. He already had a perfect plan. He just wanted to see what the disciples would do when he called them to the task.

What they did at first is what most of us do. They did the same thing Peter did when he was halfway to Jesus on the water. Peter took his eyes off Jesus and began to focus on the size of the waves. The disciples took their eyes off Jesus and began to count heads, pennies, and biscuits. You and I too often trust in the laws of the natural world, even when we are indwelled by the supernatural.

What we should do is look to Jesus and simply trust him. Instead, we try to overcome the obstacles ourselves. You may not even realize it, but your life may be defined by a paradigm of seeking newer and better strategies to succeed, strategies that do not include bent knees and folded hands in the presence of God. The most common of these strategies include, but are certainly not limited to, the following.

Moving the boundary stones.

Ancient properties did not have the benefit of modern surveys and fences to mark their perimeter. So, instead, often a row of evenly spaced stones served as the only visual (and legal) boundary.

Sometimes an enterprising landowner would arise late at night and move the entire row of stones over just slightly, a foot or two, to help himself to a little more pasture. Six months later he might do it again, hoping his neighbor wouldn't catch on. Eventually, he might earn some real acreage. This dishonest practice is known as moving the boundary stones. The Old Testament law specifically forbade it.

And though now our properties have fences and legal titles to prevent encroachment, moving the boundary stones is still one of the most commonly practiced methods of getting more of what we need or want. When we're short on time, what do we do? Give our employers seven hours and forty-five minutes instead of eight. Drive nine miles an hour over the speed limit. Stay up later and get up earlier. Cut back on the precious moments with our spouses and children in order to "get things done." A lifestyle defined by these kinds of "adjustments" is not a life centered on God.

What about money? We always need more money. So we fudge, just a little, on the tax forms. We can't tithe this month, but next month we will for sure. Get a friend to burn a CD of that expensive software package. Charge a few extra meals and miles to the expense account. Change the channel when a starving child looks to you for assistance. Swipe the credit card one more time.

If you move the boundary stones while working at the bank, they call it embezzlement. If you do it with your private finances, it's still embezzlement—from God or whomever else you are short-changing.

My son was two when we celebrated Christmas. I reveled in the experience of watching him discover and open his gifts. "Sit down right here and play, Daddy." He said this four thousand times that day as we played with his favorite gift, a new cash register. Inside the drawer are numerous plastic coins and currency. It pretends to scan bar codes on the fake groceries. It even comes with two "credit cards" that meet with instant approval when swiped properly. Ryan must have charged a fortune because all he wanted to do was swipe those cards and watch the Approved! sign pop up.

Like my son, you and I want the life where we have unlimited credit to buy whatever we want. We move the financial boundary stones by living not within the means of what God has provided but instead by burying ourselves deeper into debt. How much time do you allow God to sit down with you and your cash register? God is eager to provide what we need, if only we would ask and wait for his solution.

Moving the boundary stones goes beyond time and money. Feeling underappreciated? Tell the story about the big one that got away. Not getting enough sex? A thousand channels and Web sites await. Want more fame? Sell a little bit of your soul. Need that promotion? Tell a little white lie about the competition. I think you get the picture. Whatever the specific case, trying to extend your borders on one or more fronts is tiresome work. If you are weary from moving the stones, perhaps it's time to start living within the boundaries God has placed on your life and start trusting him to provide you with the things you need to succeed.

Using brute force.

If you can't get what you want by pilfering it secretly, then just come out in the open and take it. We see stunning examples of this in the headlines every day with governmental coups, bank robberies, kidnappings, and political elections. What we don't read about and are not so quick to condemn are the more subtle kinsmen to the illegal atrocities. A fist or even a voice raised in anger is a selfish and forceful attempt to gain ground without involving God in the heat of the moment.

Every day we are faced with crises, large and small, that tempt us to assume the only way out is by resorting to verbal or physical force. But we have more than human tactics in our bag of tricks. We are called to overcome a different way. We have Jesus, who understands our every need. He has a much better solution.

Jesus once returned to his hometown of Nazareth, a beautiful village situated in the highlands of northern Israel. Towering cliffs separated the eastern edge of town from the majestic plains hundreds of feet below. No doubt when Jesus was younger he took walks to the cliff's edge to survey the country he was called to bring back to himself. On this day Jesus was the guest of honor at the synagogue, and as such he preached a powerful sermon.

His message went well at first, with the hometown crowd nodding approvingly and beaming with pride that one of their own was so popular. However, when Jesus openly announced himself as the Messiah, the congregation became a mob. They were so angry that they drug him to the edge of town to throw him over the very cliffs that he had created. Jesus could have called down fire from heaven to destroy those who opposed him. But instead, the Bible says that Jesus simply walked through the crowd and went on his way. He didn't raise his voice. He didn't call on his disciples to defend him. He simply walked on.

Our culture teaches us that we can, or even that we must, take matters into our own hands when push comes to shove. Jesus shows us just the opposite. When God is the author and owner of your vision, and someone or something opposes you, you can go right through it peacefully, without resorting to anger or violence.

There are a thousand other categories of success strategies that ignore or defy God's plan for how to get from where you are to where you want to be. It doesn't matter if we successfully classify them all here. What does matter is that we willingly forfeit any lifestyle paradigm that takes our eyes off Jesus and onto other things.

Paul, a man who authored almost half of the New Testament, underwent a dramatic paradigm shift on the day he met Jesus. In response to his new way of thinking, he wrote these words:

> *Therefore as you have received Christ Jesus the Lord, walk in Him, rooted and built up in Him and established in the faith, just as you were taught, and overflowing with thankfulness.*
>
> *Be careful that no one takes you captive through philosophy and empty deceit based on human tradition, based on the elemental forces of the world, and not based on Christ.*
>
> *Colossians 2:6–8*

Perhaps the most prevalent cultural philosophy today is "You can do anything you want if you simply put your mind to it." And I cannot argue that many who have adapted this philosophy have done great things. However, our minds and our wills do not provide the true path to fulfilling our deepest and God-supported plans and dreams. He does not need our human ability. He needs our humble availability—availability to seek his will and trust him to handle the details.

In summary, let me paint a picture of the two choices you have before you when seeking success on this planet. You can either plod forward with your own plans for the future without seeking God first, spending your days marching and calculating; or you can take your innermost thoughts, desires, and dreams for the future to the feet of Jesus and let him take care of all the details. Trudge or trust.

We never finished our story with Jesus and the disciples after they finally made it across the lake. Peter sits, still wet and shivering from his unscheduled dip. The disciples are fresh with awe over the miracles they have witnessed in the past twenty-four hours. Jesus says something that ties everything together. He explains that if they had only understood the relationship between the bread served to the multitude and their hard day's night on the lake, things might have been different.

What does this mean? What could possibly connect their most recent experiences, which at first glance seem as different as night and day?

Go over the scene with me and see if you see the same thing that I do. When Jesus first saw the people on the shore, he called them "sheep without a shepherd." They needed encouragement, and they needed food. Jesus gave them both. He organized them into groups on the green grass and had them sit down by the quiet water's edge. He gently taught them the ways of righteousness.

Soon after, the disciples are shrouded in darkness and discouragement on the lake while Jesus watches from above and then walks alongside. Though afraid at first, they are soon comforted by the presence of their Savior and their God. Peter defies gravity. The disciples' hearts overflow more than the baskets of bread as they see him in a new light. And they worship him.

Sound familiar? Perhaps this will help connect the dots for you.

> The LORD is my shepherd, I shall not be in want.
> He makes me lie down in green pastures,
> he leads me beside quiet waters,
> he restores my soul.
> He guides me in paths of righteousness for his
>   name's sake.
> Even though I walk through the valley of the
>   shadow of death,
> I will not fear evil, for you are with me:

your rod and your staff, they comfort me.
You prepare a table before me
in the presence of my enemies.
You anoint my head with oil;
my cup overflows.
Surely goodness and love will follow me all the days
of my life,
and I will dwell in the house of the LORD forever.

Psalm 23

This is no accidental analogy. Jesus is making an announcement to his followers, both then and now. "I am your Shepherd. I am your Lord. Follow me, and you will get where you really want to go."

If Jesus is our shepherd, then by inference we are his sheep—a metaphor with broad ramifications. Any sheep that wants to advance forward must follow the shepherd's lead. A sheep that chooses to go his own way, apart from the shepherd and the rest of the flock, is a dead sheep.

You don't have to find the green pastures of your dreams on your own. Jesus knows the way, and he has every intention of getting you there. Occasionally you may feel that where he is leading is not where you want to go, and you may be tempted to break free and go your own way. Don't be discouraged or deceived into departure. Dark valleys and tough times are only temporary passages to better places on the other side.

Following Jesus does not mean giving up your dreams. It means allowing him to be the owner. It means trusting him to take care of the obstacles. It means following his lead even when it doesn't seem to make sense. Do this, and walking on water will be the least of your troubles.

Discussion Questions

What is your vision—your passion? In other words, what really drives you? What do you spend your time and efforts working toward?

Who owns your vision? Have you taken your passions and desires to God to see what he thinks? If you haven't, what's stopping you?

What obstacles block you from seeing your dreams come true? Have you—and if so how—moved the "boundary stones" in an effort to cheat your way to your dreams? Have you—and if so how—taken what you want or need in an unethical or immoral manner?

Do you think that the dreams you have for your life are there by chance—or do you think that God planted them there? If God planted them there, do you think he would not make your dreams grow into reality? And if God is going to make your dreams come true, how much work do you actually have to do to see them bloom into reality?

Overcoming
Your Fears

CHAPTER SIX

The timidity of the child or the savage is entirely reasonable; they are alarmed at this world, because this world is a very alarming place. They dislike being alone because it is verily and indeed an awful idea to be alone. Barbarians fear the unknown for the same reason that Agnostics worship it—because it is a fact.

—G. K. CHESTERTON

Is it dark or stormy outside right now? Are you alone? Do you frighten easily? If you answered yes to more than two of these questions, please skip this chapter and save it for a later date.

I'm half joking and half serious. I am about to lead both of us into the basement of our hearts, the place where our deepest fears reside. I want to take a flashlight and expose the things that frighten you most. But don't worry, when it's all over, I want us to come back out with a plan to clean that basement out and turn it into a playroom.

Modest anxiety, as in "I fear it may rain" is not what I mean. I'm talking about the dark fear of evil that lurks in your basement and in mine. As we descend into these dark places, I'll try to lead you gently. We'll start slowly with the top step and work our way into the farthest, darkest corner of them all.

I have a slight case of acrophobia, a fear of high places. But I still like to dream of skydiving and climbing tall mountains. I'm generally OK, but if I'm standing on the wooden suspension bridge over the thousand-foot drop in Royal Gorge, Colorado, you might see my legs shaking just a bit.

I am afraid of flying. I do not like the idea of placing my body onto a craft that has no contingency plans in the face of total mechanical failure. If my car engine dies, I pull over. If the plane engines die or a major malfunction occurs, I say good-bye. This is not comforting. I know the odds are unlikely that it will be me in the next plane crash, but it will be someone. I'm someone. So are you.

My little boy has brought an unspeakable joy to my life. However, with that joy comes unspeakable fear. I love him so much that my fears of losing him can run rampant if I let them. My mind taunts me with unwanted pictures of him wandering lost in a crowded mall or a deserted forest. The fear of fire pushes me to test the smoke detectors periodically, especially the one right outside his room. I am so afraid of losing him in a drowning that I find myself constantly double-checking the lock on the back gate that leads to the pond. I keep one eye on my two dogs at all times, hoping that they will be as docile in the future as they have been in the past. My greatest fear is that a disease will claim him, halting his healthy growth and slowly draining the life from him while I watch help-lessly from his side.

In a similar fashion, if my wife is out at night and she is late coming home, I begin to think of the horrific things that can hap-pen to a precious, beautiful woman in our age of brutal crime. I fear losing her and being left without her smile and her encourage-ment. I want her to be alive forever, always by my side.

A thousand other terrors sometimes weave their way into my otherwise peaceful life, jolting me from my comfort zone and filling me with dread. Sometimes I can shake it off quickly with, "Oh, stop it, Brian, that's the silliest thing you've ever thought." At other times, though, I am driven into either taking preventive measures or not knowing what to do.

You have fears like this too. Some you have shared with others, and some are so dark that you have never really talked about them with anyone for *fear* that they would think you were crazy. In some cases your fears have actually been realized. You have already encountered not only the fear but also the experience on the other side. And now you are left to pick up the pieces.

The people of Jesus' day were no different. They also had fears. They feared disease, accidents, inclement weather, and rampant crime. However, one fear stood uniquely apart. Chances are you have never faced this fear head-on yourself, though it can still be a powerful reality in our world.

Imagine an enemy that you cannot see. It has no shape. It could be here, or it could be behind you. It may be lurking just outside your bedroom door. It has no body, and all it wants is yours. It is a demon. Once an angel that sparkled in dazzling white garments and flew errands for the Most High God, this now-rebel follower of the devil has been cast out of heaven to await his final judgment. And in the meanwhile, he has an unquenchable thirst for his former glory. He roams the earth in search of anything that comes close. And the only place on the planet that provides relief is the human body, fashioned by and made in the image of God.

Based on Luke 8:26–38; Mark 5:1–20	*No one can pinpoint just why a demon would invade one life and not another. It might choose this person, or it might choose his next-door neighbor. In this case,*

it chose him, a man who lived along the eastern shores of the Sea of Galilee. And not only did it come, but it also brought friends. Hundreds of them. Thousands, perhaps. And all of them fought for control of this frail human body, leaving the original owner in a perilous situation.

His wits came and went. For a few brief moments each day, he was himself. During those times he would struggle to regain his composure and his life. But the evil spirits would never give him the chance. Suddenly he would find himself only an observer in his own body as they threw him into violent seizures. Sometimes he would watch his own hands pick up sharp stones and begin slicing his skin until he bled. Scars covered his whole body. No one could hear his silent screams because not even his own mouth belonged to him anymore.

His friends and family did their best to contain him. They placed him in a locked room. They shackled his hands and feet in iron chains. They paid people to stand guard and keep him from breaking loose and hurting himself or anyone else. Nothing worked. The evil spirits inside him gave him supernatural strength. Nothing could hold him. Finally, they gave up and let him go.

From there he wandered among the tombs in the hills around his village. He wore no clothes and lived outside among the elements. On rare occasions his invaders would leave him to his own mind, and he would find himself shivering and alone in the cold. His body was weak and dying. His hopes of returning to his old life were all but gone. He had almost stopped fighting. No one else cared anymore. Why should he?

This morning an exceptional storm broke out. The unwilling host of demons lay under a slender outcropping near the lake, only partially able to escape the wind and rain. He shuddered in the cold and dreamed of days gone by. The storm looked like it would last for hours when abruptly the sky cleared and the winds vanished. As if driven by yet another unseen power, he leapt to his feet and *broke out in a sprint for the shore. A boat full of men approached, and the body full of demons stopped at the sight of them.*

The man tried to turn and run away from this new power, but Jesus called out from the boat and yelled for him to stop. A tug-of-war began in his soul that he would never forget. His body seemed to lurch in both directions until finally the voice of Jesus drew him like a magnet. The spirits threw him onto the ground in front of Jesus and screamed.

"What do you want with me, Son of the Most High God?! Please don't torture me!" With that, the man seized and writhed in fitful tremors.

"What is your name?" Jesus asked. He could not answer, but the demons answered for him. "Legion, my Lord. For many of us live here." The spirits knew that their time was short, but they continued to negotiate with Jesus for a home other than hell. Jesus called to heaven and sent them away into a nearby herd of pigs, which immediately drowned themselves in the lake—driven mad by the spirits.

As those same restless souls left their victim broken and naked, Jesus knelt down and clothed his body with his own cloak. He held the scarred face in his hands and washed it with the lake water. He spoke gently to him and encouraged him to return to his family back in the village. For the first time in many years, the man was no longer alone. He understood. He felt in control. And he no longer felt afraid.

Jesus spoke again. "I'm sorry. We were interrupted earlier. Let me ask again. What is your name?"

The sound of his own name must have echoed somewhere in his mind as the realization struck that he could once again be himself. He no longer had a reason to be afraid.

AT THE FEET OF JESUS

You may have had the good fortune to escape demon possession in this sense. But still, all around you are voices and fears that try to control you and drain the joy from your life. Sometimes you are free from their influence, but many times you are not.

Perhaps even now you are terrified that you will give in to their sway and never be the same again. Possibly you already have. Maybe you feel now like our friend in the hills did before Jesus rescued him.

You are all alone.

Fears can drive you into unwanted solitude. Our demon-possessed friend lived by himself in lonely places. His only human companionship was rotting corpses in the tombs he frequented. His former friends and neighbors would occasionally catch a glimpse of him wandering alone in the hills. In our society it isn't that easy to notice when someone else is alone. Sometimes we don't even realize our fears have isolated us.

Loneliness can make you afraid. Fear can make you feel alone. Put the two together, and you have a dangerous combination. All across our nation and world, we have children who feel alone because they are afraid their parents do not love them either because they are too busy to be involved or because they have left the house for good. To overcome this loneliness our nation's sons are turning to violence. Our daughters seek premature sexual companionships in an effort to keep someone nearby.

The woman who once stood confidently by her husband and said "I do" now cowers in the corner, hoping and praying that he doesn't strike her or the children tonight. Her husband's actions say he does not love her, and she feels she cannot tell anyone about the private horrors of what happens at home. In a house that stands five feet from unknowing neighbors, she is more alone than ever.

Prison inmates are alone by design, but it does not change the need they have for companionship and love. Society simply shrugs and says, "But they deserve it." Jesus was so concerned about the isolation of those in prison that he once pointed out that the Christians in our society should be partially defined by their ministry to those behind bars.

Hospitals have open doors, but still they are prisons for many. Children and adults alike live every day there—some told that they will never go home again. Those of us who are fortunate enough not to call the hospital our home are so repulsed by the loneliness of life on the inside that we deliberately avoid visiting those inside for fear we will somehow be sucked inside.

Somewhere there is an older woman tucking her clothes away for the first time in the little room at the end of a nursing home hallway. A teenager who lived a few miles from where I work now faces the world alone because his father murdered his mother and little brother. A man who gave the best years of his life to his high school sweetheart sits on the couch and stares blankly at the apartment full of cardboard boxes. A single mother is overwhelmed by bills and the jobs that cannot pay them. The autistic child trapped inside a mind overwhelmed by sensory input is cared for by exhausted parents who cannot explain to their friends just how difficult their lives have become. The homeless man who moved to this country with a dream of riches now dreams only of an empty bus stop with a bench to sleep on. A young girl in an orphanage goes to sleep hoping that tomorrow someone will want to take her home.

I could go on, but I don't think I have strength left after thinking about all of these people and their situations. It's tough enough to deal with my own bouts with loneliness and fear. I don't like feeling alone. No one does.

So what should we do when we feel alone? Exactly what the man possessed by demons did. If he could do what he did in his state, then surely we can too.

What did he do? He ran to Jesus. Though the demons inside of him tried with all of their might to run in the other direction, he fought his way to the only person capable of helping him get free.

A few nights ago I awoke to the sound of my son standing at the door to our bedroom and crying and calling my name. It was one o'clock in the morning. I picked him up and began walking him back to his room when he said, "No, Daddy. I sleep your bed." Ryan never gets up in the middle of the night, so I knew something wasn't quite right. I held him close and asked him what was wrong. He pointed back down the hallway toward his room and said, "It's dark back there." Even at his tender age, my son already feels alone and afraid in the dark. He came to the only person he thought could make him feel better. And I did. Soon he was sleeping peacefully.

God's heart has a special place for the lonely. He understands how you feel, and he will not turn you away. It doesn't matter if your condition is your fault or someone else's. You won't look any worse to Jesus than a naked, bleeding, demon-possessed man exposed to the elements. Jesus can restore you to your right mind too.

Shortly after Jesus sent the demons away, the man asked Jesus if he could join him and the other disciples. Jesus had a better idea. He told the man to return home and tell others about how his life had been changed. The man who once lived in isolation now held the attentive ears of people from all over as he shared his story. He was no longer alone.

God has a special place in his heart for the lonely. He will hear your prayer for comfort and relief from your trials. Don't be afraid to ask. And when he does comfort you, he will provide people in your life to restore you to full mental and emotional health. Then you will understand why you suffered, because you now have a special gift. You will have the privilege of sharing the comfort you received from God with others who are still going through similar trials.

> Blessed be the God and Father of our Lord Jesus
> Christ, the Father of mercies and the God of all comfort.
> He comforts us in all our affliction, so that we may be
> able to comfort those who are in any kind of affliction,
> through the comfort we ourselves receive from God.
> 2 Corinthians 1:3–4

You are not in control.

Many of us fear losing control of our lives. One of my reasons for never considering the armed forces as a career choice is that I didn't want someone else telling me what to do every day. I wanted to control when I woke up and what I ate. Of course, I just got a job somewhere else, and now my boss tells me what to do for most of the day.

Demons take control of your body and your life. The man possessed certainly did not want to live alone among caves and tombs, but his demons drove him there. He did not want to scream and curse and convulse, but he couldn't help it. He was trapped inside, longing for the day he could once again choose where to go and what to do.

I like to be in control. You probably do too. And when we're not, we feel helpless. To protect us from loss of control, we build defenses—walls around our lives. When someone or something else encroaches on those walls, we fight back.

For example, let's say you like to control your time. You schedule your calendar with great care. You say no to activities that could interfere with your plans or take up too much time. You are always looking for just one more shortcut on your drive to work. You synchronize your watch with the atomic clock in Colorado, and you cannot understand why others don't. Your birthday is a stinging reminder of just how short your life is. You fear that time will run out before you see and do everything on your list.

This kind of fear can cause you to have a short fuse with those who are not punctual. If your spouse or children don't follow your rigid schedule, you react in anger or disrespect. You become tense and worrisome when deadlines approach. You become a slave to the second hand.

There's nothing wrong with being punctual, but you can go overboard. When what you seek to control becomes an obsession, it controls you. Time, food, money, people, possessions—all of these things can become idols that enslave us and control us.

But sometimes you lose control through no fault of your own. Your children reject your moral standards and break your heart. Your retirement account depreciates in an unexpected recession. A flood destroys your home. An accident cripples you. The spouse you gave your heart to now says he doesn't want it anymore.

What do you do when you lose control? What do you do when the fear of losing control petrifies you?

When Jesus restored the demonized man to his right mind, the locals did not see this as a positive move. They saw only the economic loss of the herd of pigs and the terrifying winds of change. The crazy naked man was familiar to them, and now he was gone. The one they tried to control with chains and guards no longer needed either. The townspeople felt they had lost control of the familiar, and they begged Jesus to go away.

Jesus honored their request. He got back into his boat and went to the other side of the lake. I am certain that if these countrymen had asked Jesus to stay, he would have.

If you want to be the one in control of your life, Jesus will politely step back and allow you to do so—or at least to try. God will never force himself on you. He will not stay where he is not wanted.

Sometimes when I am dressing my son, he wants to help. No problem. I like for him to help. I eventually want him to learn to dress himself. But occasionally he pushes me away entirely. "No, I do it. I put my shoes on." I humor him. I step away and watch him try to put his shoes on by himself. He grunts and groans for a few moments and then looks at me with pleading eyes. "You do it, Daddy."

Those are the words our Father longs to hear. "You do it, Daddy."

In practical terms this means that you must learn to let God take control of the things you want to control yourself. God must be the author of your schedule—all of it. Your children and their behavior are best left in God's hands, so pray as much as you discipline. Your retirement doesn't depend on the market. God will take care of you. He has more interest in your account than you ever will in this economy. You may not be able to change the heart of your spouse, but God can. If you lose your house or your job or your ability to move your legs, God will take control if you ask him to. Don't push him away when things get difficult. That's when you need him the most.

When God is in control of every aspect of your life, you have nothing to fear. God will never lose control. And he will only relinquish it to one person who demands it—you. Who would you rather have in charge?

You have no hope left.

No clothes were on his body. No chains could hold him. Nobody wanted to deal with him anymore. No amount of mental power could regain control of his arms and legs. Alone and overpowered for so long by so many forces, this man lost all hope. He feared he would never be normal again.

The dictionary definition of *hope* is something like this: "a confident wish." You use the word *wish* when you want something but probably don't expect to get it. You use the word *hope* when you want something and you are confident that you will get it. When you lose your confidence, you lose your hope.

I heard a story once about laboratory rats. Scientists placed the rats in a tub of water with no escape, forcing the creatures to swim until they drowned from exhaustion. On average the rats lasted seven hours.

However, on occasion a scientist would take one rat out of the water briefly and then put it back. The average swim time of these rats jumped to nearly three times that of the others. What made the difference?

Scientists concluded that hope was the only answer. The rescued rats believed they might be rescued again.

Humans are no different. Our hearts need hope to survive in this world. We need to *know* there is a way out of our plight.

When a doctor tells you there is no hope, what do you do? When you see the stack of bills on your left and the bank statement on the right, do you see nothing but hopelessness in between?

My dad once offered a piece of advice that has stayed with me through the years. "When all else fails, read the instructions." In other words, after you have tried putting something together your way and it didn't work, follow the steps in the owner's manual.

God is our owner, and he has provided a manual for getting you past your hopelessness.

I am able to do all things through Him who strengthens me.

Philippians 4:13

No matter what fear has brought you to despair, God says that his strength is all the power you need to get back on track.

Discussion Questions

What are your greatest fears? Why do these things scare you? How have these fears affected your life for the negative? For the positive?

Loneliness is more than just being by yourself for a few moments. Describe your fears of being alone (without friends, without a mate, without children, without someone to love you, without God). What steps have you taken in your life to avoid being alone in these areas? How has God provided relationships in your life to keep you from being alone?

What areas of your life do you feel like you must be in control of? In what areas of your life have you lost control? How does losing control of something important to you affect you? Are there areas of your life that you need to give up control to God? What are they?

What is the most hopeless you have ever felt? What made you (or now makes you) feel so hopeless? How do you think your life would be different if you had hope again? Reread Philippians 4:13 and describe how God promises you hope in your situation?

Cultivating a Thankful Heart

CHAPTER SEVEN

Gratitude unlocks the fullness of life. It turns what we have into enough, and more. It turns denial into acceptance, chaos to order, confusion to clarity. It can turn a meal into a feast, a house into a home, a stranger into a friend. Gratitude makes sense of our past, brings peace for today, and creates a vision for tomorrow.

—MELODY BEATTIE

The truth of the matter is that I just hate to mow the grass. It's time-consuming, and it's *work*. I've been mowing since I was seven years old, helping my dad with our own yard. By the time I was fourteen, I had my own lawn-mowing enterprise with ten to fifteen yards to mow each week. And now that I think about it, I can't remember a single lawn mower that didn't occasionally give me fits trying to get it started. I would prime and pull and then pout when it wouldn't cooperate. My whole life has been plagued with lawn-mowing madness.

I had one client with the mother of all mowings. Her yard was more than two acres, much larger than the size of mine now. Her tiny home covered only a fraction of the land, leaving most of the plot to my plodding. My lawn mower was a self-propelled edition with a twenty-inch blade, only the self-propel was on vacation.

A steep drainage ditch running the length of a football field separated her yard from the neighbor's. Though ninety-seven years old, this kind widow demanded sternly that the ditch be mowed in its entirety. If I was lucky, and the lawn mower started on the first try, it would take me only a mere three hours to earn my fifteen dollars.

My dad would drop me off, start the lawn mower, and make sure I got going. Afterward, I would mow until the engine halted in protest for more of its favorite beverage. This is when I held my breath. I would fill up the gas tank, reach down, and say a prayer that the engine would turn on the first pull. As usual, it did not. I pulled again. And again. And again. I pulled until exhaustion took over, and then I sat in the grass hoping my father would come by to check on me.

While sitting there in the grass one day, feeling sorry for myself, I heard a voice call my name. I looked up to see the waving neighbor on the other side of the ditch. He was walking away from me down his driveway with what I couldn't help but notice was a large and inviting glass of lemonade. Mr. Herring was a kind man now in his early fifties. I watched him walk away, and I quietly mumbled to God and myself that it sure would be nice if I had a glass of lemonade that big. I reached down to pluck a spot of uncut grass, figuring that was the only way I would now finish this large yard, when I heard a simple but stirring sound that I will never forget.

Mr. Herring, having reached the end of his driveway near the street, turned onto the small wooden bridge spanning the drainage ditch and now walked across it. His shoes and the old weatherbeaten boards met together, clapping together slowly in a distinctive rhythm. I looked up to realize that he was coming over to see about me. I looked once more at the glass of lemonade and wondered if perhaps that was for me. Glancing now at his other hand, he held a screwdriver and pair of pliers. When Mr. Herring finally reached me, I stood to shake hands with him. He greeted me warmly, handed me the glass of lemonade, and knelt down to look at my lawn mower. "Let's see what we can do about this."

I have no idea what Mr. Herring did down there on his knees. I just know that by the time I finished my lemonade, which didn't take more than a few seconds, that old mower was ready for another round. He smiled, and we chatted briefly, and he was back across the little bridge, waving all the while. I can't say I was all that happy to be mowing again, but I was grateful for the drink and the lawn-side assistance.

What makes this story most memorable to me is that it repeated itself over and over again. I mowed that yard for four more years, and almost every time I had trouble with that stubborn lawn mower. And even when I didn't, when I paused to refill the gas tank, Mr. Herring was out of his house and walking across that old bridge, always with a giant glass of lemonade. Sometimes when I finished the job, he would invite me over to his house for a snack.

Why was Mr. Herring so nice to me? Mr. Herring was a member of my church and a former Sunday school teacher. He bought my first real Bible as a birthday present when I was eleven years old. In fact, he bought all of the guys in his class a Bible on their birthdays. Mr. Herring apparently did more than teach the Bible. He did more than give away Bibles. He *lived* the Bible, and to him part of living it was to help other people who were in a jam—even ungrateful young teenagers mowing the yard next door. Now, as I write these words to you, I cannot help but think I should be more grateful for all that God has done for and given to me.

I don't have the Bible that Mr. Herring gave to me nearly twenty-five years ago, but I do have his example. In the Bible is a story. In honor of Mr. Herring, I would like to share that story because it reminds me to be grateful in my world of ingratitude.

Based on
Luke 17:10−17

He knew he was in trouble when he noticed the tingling in his fingertips, accompanied by dry, white patches on his hands. He lay on his bed in the moments just before dawn, wondering when to tell his wife. "My life is over," he whispered dreadfully to himself. "I am losing my family, my friends, my job."

His wife screamed when she told him. She screamed and cried and cursed. She paced, even ran, around the room, wanting at once to hold her husband and to run from him in fear that she, too, would contract the disease. His children huddled in the corner, not old enough to understand why Daddy had to move away. They cried and begged him to stay, but he knew that he could never hold them again. His heart sank as he walked away with a bed mat and change of clothes. He wanted to look back, but he couldn't.

He saw the morning crowd beginning their day, chatting busily and bustling towards work. He nearly stumbled in despair when he realized what he now had to do. Clearing his throat and taking a weak gasp of air, he shouted, "Unclean! Unclean!!" Everyone within earshot stopped and stared. Was this a joke? Was Elijah kidding? The look on his face answered their questions. The crowd parted quickly. Mothers grabbed their children and ran. Grown men tripped over themselves to make way. Elijah's eyes did not meet theirs. Instead, between a wall of fear on either side, he stared at the ground and continued his journey to the edge of his village where the leper community lived.

Elijah saw them in the distance. The smoke from their breakfast fire wafted lazily toward him in the morning breeze. They looked up at him as he approached and then looked back down at the fire. Their conversation ceased. They all thought the same thing. *"Not another one. We barely have enough to support our-selves. And this guy is one of them."*

Elijah's home was a border town along the line that divides Galilee of the Jews from the country of Samaria. Elijah was him-self a decent and upstanding Samaritan citizen. The leper colony was purely Jewish, nine men who fled their home to seek refuge and pity from their foreign neighbors. Their own countrymen con-sidered them cursed and rejected forever by God and would rarely offer assistance. The Samaritans were much more likely to help.

The nine men didn't want another, much less a Samaritan, but what could they say? Desperate times have produced stranger bed-fellows than this. The Samaritans provided their livelihood, if that's what you could call this meager existence. So they welcomed him hesitantly and introduced him to the makeshift colony where he would live, and eventually die, as a leper.

The days turned into weeks, then months, and finally years. At first Elijah's wife left food for him on the edge of town. The cou-ple would shout to each other from a hundred yards away. She would often bring one of the children with her so that Elijah could watch his children grow. The visits began to grow less frequent, and his family became accustomed to living without him. Out of sight and out of his mind from loneliness and despair, Elijah longed to see his wife and children—to hold and kiss them and stroke the hair from their eyes with his fingers, what was left of them. His hopelessness could be no greater.

Late one afternoon Elijah sat, staring at the distant cliffs of Nazareth. All I have to do is climb up there and jump, and it's all over, *he thought. Staring northward, he seriously began to plan the trek up the mountains of Galilee in order to take his own life.*

Elijah stood to return to his tent when he noticed another group of men headed his way. They were at least a mile off, but he could hear shouting from others nearby. "He's coming! The

Nazarene is coming! Jesus is coming to town. Make way!" Jesus—could it be? The other lepers heard the shouting as well and bolted from their tents. "Did they say Jesus?" Elijah nodded and pointed to the approaching men. Elijah had heard that Jesus was a healer, that he had even healed a leper once. Would Jesus have the power, or the interest, to heal him?

He looked at his friends. The ten of them exchanged knowing glances, and all at once they began to run. They ran like they were teenagers again, shouting "Unclean" all the way. In just a moment they reached a safe distance and stopped. Each leper strained his eyes to see if he could identify Jesus, but all of the newcomers looked the same. They stood and wondered just what to do next. They didn't want to go closer in their condition, but they longed to see if Jesus would—and could—heal them.

One of the Jews in Elijah's group shouted, "Jesus, Master, please have compassion on us!" The disciples stopped. Jesus did not. He kept walking toward them. Now Elijah knew which one was Jesus. He held his breath, hoping for the best but expecting nothing when Jesus spoke: "Go and present yourself to the priests."

Elijah, though not a Jew, knew what these words meant. If a leper has been healed, he is required by Jewish law to have the healing confirmed by an official priest. He and the other men looked at their hands and their skin. They didn't feel or seem any different, but who were they to question the Master? Off they went, running excitedly toward a nearby Jewish village.

Several minutes into the run, all ten men halted in unison. Each felt a tingle in his hands and feet and looked to see fresh pink skin where once only dry, white patches had lived. Missing fingers and toes reappeared. Sensations returned. Shouting and screaming for joy, they all began the run again—this time in a dead sprint to have their healing approved by the priest. All of them except Elijah. He stood rooted in shock, still eyeing his new shell with awe. He looked up at his friends of several years as they disappeared in a cloud of dust ahead, then back toward his village and the small band of visitors headed toward it.

Overcome with a sense of indescribable gratitude, Elijah could think of nothing but Jesus. The priests could wait. This couldn't. He turned around and ran with all of his might back to Jesus. And this time he didn't stop a safe distance away. He caught up with the weary travelers, shouting praises to God all the while. Jesus and his disciples stopped and turned toward him. Elijah blew past all twelve disciples before they had time to react. On reaching Jesus, he leapt into a slide that would make any baseball coach proud, right into home plate at the feet of Jesus. Tears and thank-yous poured from him at an uncontrollable pace.

Jesus smiled and drank in the man's appreciation fully. He looked up again, expecting to see the other men, formerly known as lepers, close behind. But there were none. Jesus rose to his toes, looking over his disciples to be sure, but no one else was coming. Elijah was the only one.

"I counted ten men healed of leprosy. Why is it that now only one man returned to acknowledge me as the author of their healing? You would think my brothers, the Jews, would be the first to offer thanks. But this foreigner . . ."

Looking down at Elijah, Jesus knelt and placed his hands on his head, something no one had done to Elijah in a long, long time. "Elijah, you may rise to your feet! Your faith in me has saved not only your skin but also your soul."

Elijah couldn't believe his ears. He stood, wiping the tears from his eyes and thanking Jesus once more before breaking out in a dead sprint for home. The priests could wait until tomorrow.

Imagine Elijah's life from this day forward. Early each morning he wiggles his fingers and toes wildly, thanking God for all twenty of them. Firm handshakes with business associates and friends are now small treasures. Tender evening moments with his children are cherished as he tucks them away. He playfully dances with his wife before whisking her away to bed. Every day is new, filled with unending gratitude.

I'm attracted to people like Elijah, those who have a childlike celebration for the smallest things in life. Their contentment is contagious.

You and I can experience that kind of contentment, and we don't have to wait until we lose something before we realize just how precious it is. An attitude of gratitude is all it takes, and the thankful leper's experiences teach us how to develop one.

Thank is a transitive verb.

Go back with me to grade school English. A transitive verb needs nouns on either side of it to operate correctly. I thank you. You thank me. An intransitive verb requires only one noun on the left side. I sleep. You run. They wait. Get the picture? Gratitude does not, and cannot, exist without the thank-er and the thank-ee meeting head-on. You can't just thank. You have to thank someone.

I stress this point because our world increasingly misses this principle. As I write these words, Thanksgiving Day is two days away. On television this week I have seen children's programs, sitcoms, and news specials encourage viewers to be thankful. I have watched curbside interviews as talk-show hosts ask, "What are you thankful for this year?" They don't even realize that they've left out the right side of the equation altogether. Thankfulness needs a recipient. God is the bearer of all blessings, and common sense tells us that he is the rightful beneficiary of our gratitude.

The ten lepers were undoubtedly thankful for what Jesus did for them, but only one took the time and effort to make the return trip and openly air his feelings. Any gratitude felt internally by the others never made its way back to Jesus and is for all practical purposes nonexistent. Like a tree that falls in the forest out of earshot, unexpressed gratitude does not make a sound—or a difference.

I was a senior in high school. Chris was a freshman. Chris was shy, skinny, and unsure of himself in social settings. I watched other students, including friends of mine, torture Chris simply because they had nothing better to do. Because I once was like Chris, I knew all too well how he felt. I decided that I would do my best to treat him differently than most others. My goal was simple: I wanted him to know that I thought he was a valuable human being. I didn't do much. I just treated him with basic respect whenever he was around.

My year with Chris came and went, and I went off to college. I didn't think much about him anymore. Then one day I ran into his parents at a shopping mall. I waved from a distance. His mother waved me over. Curious to know why a near stranger would want to speak with me, I obliged. She looked at me seriously and said simply, "I just want to thank you, for Chris." Then she continued on her way.

A few years later, at that same mall, I ran into Chris himself. He was out of high school, much taller, and much stockier. He ran over to me and, in so many words, thanked me as well. Though neither he nor his parents told me exactly what they were thankful for, I knew. And their gratitude meant more to me than I could ever explain. To this day when I am tempted to disregard or disrespect another human being, I think of Chris and the difference I made in his life. It reminds and encourages me to love the underdog.

It's nice to be on the receiving end of a hearty thank-you, isn't it? It changes you, lifts you up, makes you more likely to keep up the good work. It's a plain fact; humans benefit when they hear honest words of appreciation, but they aren't the only ones.

God, too, is profoundly moved by gratitude when his children choose to share their feelings with him. Jesus was so moved by the one leper's response that he conferred on him a healing of not only the body but also the soul.

Just as my heart is touched when my son offers a voluntary "Thank you, Daddy" for his juice, so is the heart of God moved when you honestly offer your thanks for the good things he has given you in your life.

So don't hold out and don't hold back. Let God and the people around you who deserve your gratitude *hear* from you. Tell them how you feel. Write a letter or send a thank-you card to the people who have made a positive difference in your life. Count your blessings—name them one by one—and acknowledge God as the source for each.

Gratitude is as important as obedience.

Jesus told the lepers to go. All but one did. He did not go. In fact, he ran in the opposite direction. No one told him to come to Jesus. No one told him to shout praises. No one told him to fall down on the ground and say thanks. And yet Jesus does not commend the nine for their obedience. He commends the one for his unprompted gratitude.

Church pews are filled weekly with people who are doing the right thing. They do not curse or steal from their employers or cheat on their taxes. They give money and time to the cause of Christ. They read their Bibles and pray several times each week. They have basic integrity. And yet, if you studied the sullen faces that many of them wear, you would wonder why people who supposedly sit in the presence of God are so sad. I think it is largely because these lives of obedience often fail to acknowledge the fresh touches from God that come every day and to say a simple thank-you for them.

It's easy to get lost in the discipline of obedience without really connecting with the one we are obeying. Human nature doesn't lend itself to gratitude. It lends itself to griping.

If I were to spend an evening with your closest friends, family, and coworkers, would they say you are grateful or grumpy? Be careful before answering. These people see you every day. Some of them live with you. They've heard your reaction to the waiter when your food order is wrong. They've watched your face when the boss handed you yet another unexpected emergency project. They know what you become when your pet peeves proliferate. A handful of these people know who you really are before the caffeine and makeup begin to smooth over the rough edges.

A grumpy attitude can evolve quickly and quietly into a sour character. You unknowingly become one of those people no one wants to be around because you are always in protest. Never happy with the way things are, you only complain about the way things could and should be. Before you know it, even you don't want to be around you.

If this sounds like your life, then you have a case of the grumps. It's time to let them go. How? I'll give you the exact formula. Ready? It's a four-letter word. See if you can spot it in the verse below.

> *Happy are the meek,*
> *because they will inherit the earth.*
> > *Matthew 5:5, author's paraphrase*

Meek

If a dictionary publisher called you and asked you to render a picture to accompany the word *meek* in their next edition, what would you draw? Because this word is underused, your brain probably attempts to find the closest match to a word you use more often. *Weak* is the word that comes to your mind. Correspondingly, your image of meekness leans toward something feeble or ineffectual.

Not so. Take your picture, crumple it into a ball, and throw it into the nearest wastebasket. Just because *meek* and *weak* can work together in poetry does not mean they walk the same path in meaning. Generally speaking, to be weak is to be willing but unable, while to be meek is to be able but unwilling. A meek person exercises restraint by not complaining in less than ideal situations, even though she is able and the situation warrants. You'll find the meek overlooking insult and provocation and offering compliments and blessings in return. They are a rare breed. You don't see them often, but they are out there. You've seen them in action, and you privately long for their strength and resolve. You want to know their secret.

You can be meek, too, if you hold on to the promise of Jesus. The meek—those who patiently and thankfully accept everything that happens to them as part of God's plan—will inherit the earth. In English this means that your reward is coming. Your restraint and goodwill are not invisible to the eyes of God. Those who try and take the world for themselves today will be surprised to watch Jesus one day hand it over to the meek.

Meekness is the foundation for gratitude. As you walk with Jesus on your journey through life, keep this in mind. Obedience is not all God seeks from you. He can easily create a race of robots that never disobey his commands, but he wants more. He wants you to choose to pause in your obedience and run back to him with open expressions of heartfelt appreciation for all he has done for you.

Giving thanks is for all seasons.

Tomorrow my in-laws will arrive for an extended Thanks-giving stay. Still, in the midst of this dark hour, I am grateful. I'm kidding, of course. I love my wife's parents. They provide warmth and love to our holiday and our home, not to mention the fudge and free baby-sitting.

In all seriousness, there are times when it becomes difficult to think of thanksgiving. One of the most difficult verses in the Bible for me to live by is 1 Thessalonians 5:18:

> *Give thanks in everything,*
> *for this is God's will for you*
> *in Christ Jesus.*

In all circumstances? What about now? Surely I'm exempt tonight as my wife and I mourn the loss of an unborn child in a miscarriage. Certainly the families of those lost in the terrorist attacks on New York City during the sunrise of the twenty-first century cannot be expected to feel gratitude. It's ludicrous.

Notice that God did not say, "Give thanks *for* every circum-stance." We are not required to thank God for tragedy. However, God does say that we may, and should, offer him thanks for what we can while we experience tragedy. And before you say, "That's just not possible," please note that God never asks us to do what he hasn't already done himself. Jesus faced tremendous sorrow and pain in his life many times, but often in the middle of his most difficult times he chose to thank God anyway. And it made all the difference.

When Jesus saw a hungry multitude to feed and only a small boy's lunch with which to do it, he did not complain or lose hope.

He thanked his Father for the little that he did have, and God fed them all.

Standing at the tomb of his close friend Lazarus, weeping openly, Jesus thanked God for taking the time to listen to his prayer. Moments later Lazarus walked out alive and well.

The night before he died, Jesus gave thanks twice at a dinner for the food and drink that symbolized his approaching agony. Three days later he walked out of his tomb alive, never to die or experience pain again.

See the pattern? In the face of tremendous pressure to choose despair, fear, or bitterness, thanksgiving rearranges the apparent plot of the story and creates a surprise ending.

This pattern exists throughout the life of Jesus and in the rest of the Bible, giving us numerous examples to follow. In the Old Testament there is a short but powerful story about how gratitude miraculously altered the course of events. If you have a Bible nearby, take the time to read 2 Chronicles 20. It won't take you long. When the politically fractured and weak nation of Israel was about to be overrun by numerous approaching armies, God's children marched out to meet them unarmed. As they went, they sang songs of thanksgiving to the Lord. The result? The invading armies "coincidentally" became confused and began killing one another. By the time the Israelites arrived at the battlefield, every enemy soldier was dead.

God hears and honors gratitude. It is God's will that you develop a character that instinctively appreciates him, regardless of the circumstances. He wants you to trust him more than you trust your senses and your feelings. The next time you find yourself ready to complain, bite your tongue and take a deep breath. Let it out slowly. Then look around. Look past all of the things you don't like and find at least one thing that you do. Thank God for that, and you may be surprised at what God does to change the apparent ending of your story.

Discussion Questions

Are you a complainer? Do you gripe and mumble? If so, do you feel better or worse during one of your gripe sessions? What has complaining really gained you in terms of being a happier, more joyful person?

Who are you thankful for in your life? Have you expressed the full extent of your gratitude to them? Why not? What is stopping you from writing a letter or making a phone call right now? How can you thank God for all of the blessings he has provided you?

Describe the areas of your life where you have been obedient to God. Which are you more likely to be in your relationship with God—obedient or grateful? Based on this chapter's definition of the word *meek,* are you meek? What can you do today to become more meek and thankful?

Sometimes—perhaps even now—life seems too hard to be thankful. Whether those events are past or present, you still have things you can be grateful for. What are they? Count your blessings. Name them one by one.

Getting Through the Grief

CHAPTER EIGHT

Grief is a tidal wave that overtakes you,
smashes down upon you with unimaginable force,
sweeps you up into its darkness,
where you tumble and crash against unidentifiable surfaces,
only to be thrown out on an unknown beach, bruised, reshaped. . . .
Grief will make a new person out of you,
if it doesn't kill you in the making.

—STEPHANIE ERICCSON

I hate death.

My idealism and its reality are forever locked in a ferocious wrestling match. I am resolved to keep it as distant from me as possible, but every day it grows stronger, and I grow weaker. I know that I cannot escape it, though with all my might I will delay its victory and pray that Jesus comes before it claims me.

Death is everywhere. It hides around dark corners and snatches the unprepared away. It sometimes brushes close by, taking someone I know. In the past month alone I've watched it mercilessly claim the life of an innocent two-year-old in a drowning, a prominent local pastor, one of my son's Bible study teachers at church, a teenager who committed suicide, and a family member.

I just came back from the funeral of an uncle. My father, one of nine children, just lost the first of his siblings to death's grip. I did not know Virgil Shipman well, but the memories I have are fond. I attended the funeral as much to support my father as I did to pay respects to my uncle.

I arrived early from out-of-town to the family luncheon and paced uncomfortably in the small and overheated Oklahoma church fellowship hall. Soon relatives I had not seen in twenty-five years began to stream inside, huddled in warm coats to protect against January winds. My parents greeted me in hushed tones.

More than sixty of us huddled around tables and chatted quietly over lunch. I sat with a favorite cousin from my youth and tried to catch up. I was just pausing between the fried chicken and the chocolate cake when a dark-suited stranger slipped quietly through the back door and motioned for my cousin and me to come with him.

Curious, I rose and followed. As we walked through the back of the church and toward an open doorway, I cast a knowing glance at my cousin and guessed the nature of our calling. Two strong guys. An hour before the funeral. My stomach tried to turn back, but my legs prevented it.

There it was. The hearse. It was open. Virgil's casket was waiting. My cousin and I obeyed our orders and helped carry our uncle inside. I didn't count on being this close to death when I came here. I wanted to keep my distance as much as possible. Now I held it in my hands and felt its full weight. It was the first time I ever held a coffin.

We returned to our seats and resumed our reminiscing. As the hour for the service began, the conversations became notably more quiet and somber. The ministers came in and gave the family brief instructions, and we were off. My mother held my hand and asked me to help her comfort my father, who now marched somberly forward and into the sanctuary.

Once the entire family took their places and the minister began the eulogy, I couldn't help but survey the faces of the Shipman clan around me. Faces that smiled only moments ago now struggled to maintain composure. Virgil's children sobbed and sometimes cried out. His widow, much of her sorrow already spent, stared into space. My other uncles and aunts dabbed at the tears in their eyes. And then I looked at my dad. He wasn't just crying. He was weeping.

I wish I could say what happened next was out of love for my uncle, but the truth is I did not know him well enough to grieve deeply. The unexpected tears in my eyes formed in response to my father's grief. I mourned precisely because he mourned. I couldn't stand to see my father lose someone he loved so much. Not knowing what else to do, I placed my hand on my father to let him know that I was there. And there we wept together.

Death and grief are inevitable, though admittedly we bury this truth deep within our psyche to avoid it as long as possible. Only when we lose someone to its clutches does it come to the forefront of our attention—and that with a ferocity and depth known only to its closest victims.

Death was never part of God's plan for you and me. He created us to live and breathe and walk with him forever. But our stubborn wills to live apart from him have taught us all too well that there is no life apart from him. There is only death. It is not Adam and Eve's fault that we face death, but our own. We, too, have deliberately gone against the will of God in search of something better than what he has offered. And for that, we must die. A few words from the Bible seal this truth . . .

For the wages of sin is death.

Romans 6:23

It is appointed for people to die once—and after this, judgment.

Hebrews 9:27

Before we go forward and learn how to deal with and get over the grief that comes from death, let's agree together not to blame God for its sting. He is not responsible for death; we are.

Even though I know this, I still hate death. I am comforted only in knowing that Jesus hates it too. How do I know this? Jesus lost many people close to him during his days on earth, but one man in particular stands out above all the rest, his dear friend Lazarus.

| Based on |
| John 11:1–44 |

Lazarus had two sisters, Mary and Martha. All three siblings lived together in the small village of Bethany. Bethany lay just under two miles from the city of Jerusalem on the eastern slope of the Mount of Olives. This city still exists, and its present-day name is El-Azarieh.[1] Say it out loud a few times, and you will notice it sounds suspiciously like "Lazarus." This is not a coincidence. This city still remembers what happened to its patron nearly two thousand years ago.

Perhaps it started with a quiet cough followed a week later by shortness of breath. Now it was much more serious. Lazarus lay on his bed mat in his room, shivering from a high fever. Mary sat beside him, dabbing his forehead with a cool, wet cloth and

speaking gentle words of encouragement to her brother. Martha paced outside the room with heavy steps and a heart to match.

Many of Lazarus's friends sat in the living room and spoke to one another just above a whisper. Sometimes they talked about their sick friend, and sometimes they had to talk about something else. The prognosis was not good.

Early one morning during the vigil, Martha bolted out of Lazarus's room with a small sheet of parchment. She handed it to her servant and said, "Find him and give him this. He's on the other side of the Jordan. Stay on the Jericho road, and you will find him. Give him this. Please, as soon as you can!" Martha brought her hand to her mouth and tried to stop an oncoming wail, but she could not. The servant hugged her, grabbed his things, and sped through the open door.

Martha calculated that it would take one day for her servant to reach Jesus, and at least one more for Jesus to return. Two days. Would that be enough time? Should she have sent for him sooner?

Less than two hours later, Lazarus entered a rapid decline. The servant had barely cleared Jerusalem and begun the steep descent toward Jericho. Conversations turned to silence. Martha's pacing turned to praying. Mary's prayers turned to pleading.

Lazarus's breathing became labored. He slipped into unconsciousness. Mary held his hand and told him not to go, but her words were unheard. His last breath came as Martha came in to check on him. The sisters could not believe it. Their brother was gone. Their tears commingled as they fell into each other's arms and mourned.

Two days later Jesus still had not come. The sisters proceeded as planned with the funeral and buried their brother in his tomb, a small cave located just outside of the village. Hundreds of people from Jerusalem and its surrounding villages came to mourn the loss of their friend. Lazarus was laid to rest.

Two more days later, as Mary and Martha continued to grieve their loss, Jesus and his disciples arrived on the outskirts of town. Jesus was no stranger, and when others recognized his approach, they bolted for Lazarus's home to tell the sisters that Jesus had arrived. When a guest notified Martha that Jesus was here, she could think of nothing else than to be with him. "He's here!" she said to Mary, but Mary did not move. Lost in her bereavement, Mary could not bring herself to go anywhere. Martha left her and ran at once to meet Jesus.

She found him still outside the village, talking with many others about how Lazarus had taken ill and died four days ago. When Martha approached, the crowd parted for her. She saw Jesus and ran to him. Jesus could see the pain in her eyes, and it touched him. Martha spoke first.

"Jesus, if only you had been here! Lazarus would still be alive. I still know that God will do whatever you ask." Then she collapsed in Jesus' arms and wailed.

Jesus leaned Martha back and held her shoulders to steady her and said, "Martha, your brother will be alive again."

Martha had heard Jesus speak of the resurrection at the end of time and acknowledged to Jesus that she believed she would one day see Lazarus again. But, knowing it would be so long, she still continued to cry uncontrollably.

"You misunderstand me, Martha. The resurrection isn't just something that will occur at the end of time. I am the resurrection. I am life. Everyone who trusts in me will live, even though he might taste death. Whoever lives and trusts in me will never die. Do you understand? Do you trust me when I say this?"

Martha nodded. Jesus' words were comforting to her, but she still could not stop crying. She turned and ran back to the house.

When she arrived, she knelt beside Mary and said, "Our Teacher is here. He has asked to see you." Mary looked through her tears at her sister.

"He wants to see me?" Mary asked. Martha nodded. Mary stood at once and ran as fast as she could to the edge of town. It was nearing sunset, and Mary could see the red clouds in the west ahead of her as she ran. She found the crowd and made her way to Jesus. When she saw his face, she immediately fell down on her face at his feet and lamented loudly. "Lord," she said between sobs, "if only you had been here! My brother would still be alive!"

When Mary said this, Jesus' mood changed dramatically. He hung his head and looked at her, his face gloomy and withdrawn. "Where is he? Where have you put my brother Lazarus?"

"Follow us," several in the crowd volunteered, and the whole group began walking toward the tomb. Jesus reached down to help Mary up. When she stood and they began the procession, Jesus wept.

In an instant everyone was quiet, and all eyes were on Jesus. No one had ever witnessed him in tears before.

As they neared the tomb, the crowds could only guess that Jesus was mourning for Lazarus. How could they have realized that he wept because they wept? His grief erupted because of their grief— and because of the sting that death had brought to his closest friends.

Word spread and hundreds of people gathered at the tomb of Lazarus, staring blankly at the large rock that sealed its entrance. Everyone assumed that this would be a reunion of mourning, a repeat of the funeral for Jesus' sake.

All fell silent when Jesus walked forward and leaned on the stone, still wiping tears from his eyes. He stayed there for several minutes, sobbing quietly to himself. Finally, he turned to face the crowd. He motioned to several men standing to his right and said, "Take away the stone. Roll it back."

The men looked at one another, then at Jesus, and then at Martha. Martha said, "Lord, I know you want to see him one last time, but he's been dead for four days now. Roll that stone back, and we will all be driven away by the smell."

"Martha, did you not just hear my words back at the village? I told you that if you trusted in me, you would see the glory of God." Jesus looked back at the men and said, "Now take away this stone."

They didn't argue. Together they broke the seal and rolled the stone away from the opening. It was dark inside. Jesus walked directly in front of the entrance and stood there. Martha was not wrong; the smell of death was present. Noses were tucked away, but all eyes remained on Jesus as he placed one hand on the tomb's entrance and turned his eyes heavenward.

"Father," he began, "thank you. Thank you for hearing my prayers—the ones as I traveled here and the one I offer now. You always hear me. I say these things because I want those here this evening to know that you are the author of what is about to happen. Let my friends here know that you have sent me here."

With that, Jesus stood back. He took a deep breath, stared into the darkness, and lifted one hand toward the tomb. "Lazarus," he spoke with all his might. "Come out of there!"

For a few seconds nothing happened, but not an eye left the tomb opening. And though the sun was about to fade, everyone could now see the shadowy figure emerging from the tomb. Wrapped from head to toe in grave linens, Lazarus stepped forward without a word and stood in front of Jesus.

Some fell to their knees. Others lifted hands to heaven and shouted praises. Some screamed unintelligibly. At least half the crowd simply ran away at lightning speed. Mary and Martha stood paralyzed, not knowing whether to trust their eyes or wait until they could see the face of the man standing there.

"These clothes are for a dead man," Jesus said as he turned back to the crowd and placed his arm around Lazarus's shoulder. "Let's get him into something more suitable for living!"

I know, I know. It sounds crazy, but it happened. Jesus gave life to a man who had been dead. He was gone. It was over. He was out of the picture. The funeral was two days ago. He had already started to *rot*. But Jesus is not intimidated by death. He is the resurrection and the life. He has the power to give it back.

We will focus later on getting through grief by placing our hope on the future of the final resurrection and seeing our loved ones in heaven. But first I would like to go a little deeper and take a look at what happens with the grieving sisters before they see Lazarus raised. Here we see how Jesus can comfort us *now*—in the middle of our toughest times. I notice three things that Jesus did to comfort Mary and Martha before he arrived at the tomb.

God may sometimes appear to be absent.

If you read the biblical text of our story, you will see that Jesus deliberately delayed his coming to Mary and Martha. He could easily have been there sooner but chose to start his journey two full days after he received word of Lazarus's illness. Doesn't sound right, does it? Why would he do that?

Conjecture on this subject abounds, but I think it's not so complicated. I look at it as God's "moment of silence" in honor and in memory and in mourning over what has just taken place.

Like the rest of the nation and parts of the world, I grieved as I witnessed the wretched events of September 11, 2001. I watched in silence as planes full of innocent people slammed into buildings holding the same. No words could possibly come close to describing my feelings as I saw those skyscrapers collapse in an angry cloud of dust and debris. On that day our nation was silent, and for many years to come we will observe an official moment of silence on the anniversary of this tragedy. Silence is the best thing, or perhaps the only thing, that we have to offer in the shadow of something so devastating.

Likewise, we humans who are made in the image of God are doing precisely what God sometimes does. So we should not think it strange when God is not quick to rush into the middle of calamity to "fix it" or preach a rousing sermon on the future hope we have. We think death is difficult for us to deal with. Imagine what it does to the heart of a perfect, eternal God. Certainly God has a right to remain silent on such occasions.

When Jesus approached death on his cross of suffering, even he looked to heaven and said, "My God. My God! Why have you abandoned me?" In his own death Jesus faced a crisis of belief. Where was his Father? Why couldn't he sense his presence during the most difficult time of his life? As much as God hates death, watching his own Son die must have been heart-wrenching. His response was a moment of silence felt around the world.

We sometimes interpret his temporary hush as distance or apathy, though neither is true. Jesus deliberately waited to go and see his friends as part of his plan, but he did go. He gave Mary and Martha time to grieve properly, and then he approached them gently from a distance. Notice that he did not even go directly into town. Instead, he remained on the outskirts of the village and waited for word of his arrival to trickle back to the sisters. Even then, only Martha was ready to approach him. It took longer for Mary to do the same.

Your grief does not go unseen or unfelt by God. He, too, is affected profoundly by your loss. And though at first it may seem to you that God is not present for you, I assure you that he is there.

He is right beside you, and he will be glad to listen to your questions and your pain. Don't be afraid to go to him. He will hear you out, and then he will comfort you.

God's words can comfort you.

When Jesus finally did see Martha for the first time since Lazarus's death, he remained quiet until Martha took the time to voice her feelings. "Jesus, if you had only been here."

Jesus responded to her with words of comfort and encouragement: "Your brother will rise again," and "I am the resurrection and the life." We have no hope against death if we do not have these words. Our Christian brothers and sisters who precede us in death are not gone forever. We will see them again.

I found moments of comfort in my uncle's funeral. They came during the eulogy, where I was encouraged to hear that Virgil was a faithful Christian man who made a difference in the lives of those who knew him. I heard story after story about him. He was a faithful husband. He was a loving father. He had a gentle spirit. And he had a great sense of humor.

My dad and I will see Virgil again one day. Those words comfort me. I still grieve, but I also experience consolation.

You will see the Christian brother or sister you have lost recently too. That promise is yours to hold on to until you redeem it at the end of time.

God's Word is full of promises concerning the great reunion we will have at the end of time. Allow me to share just a few with you. If you have lost someone recently, make these words your own. They are God's assurance to you.

Precious in the sight of the LORD
is the death of his saints.

Psalm 116:15

Listen! I am telling you a mystery:
We will not all fall asleep,
but we will all be changed,
in a moment, in the twinkling of an eye,
at the last trumpet.
For the trumpet will sound,
and the dead will be raised incorruptible,
and we will be changed.
Because this corruptible must be clothed with
*   incorruptibility,*
and this mortal must be clothed with immortality.
Now when this corruptible is clothed with
*   incorruptibility,*
and this mortal is clothed with immortality,
then the saying that is written will take place:
Death has been swallowed up in victory.

O Death, where is your victory?
O Death, where is your sting?

Now the sting of death is sin,
and the power of sin is the law.
But thanks be to God,
who gives us the victory
through our Lord Jesus Christ!

1 Corinthians 15:51–57

God's understanding can comfort you.

Though Mary and Martha both came to Jesus in the same way, and with the same complaint, Jesus chose remarkably different methods to comfort each of them. With Martha, Jesus used words. With Mary, he chose weeping.

Neither my mother nor I had the words to say to comfort my father at his brother's funeral. But we wept with him. It was all we could do.

God is not immune to sadness. He is not passive to the pain that you feel. He understands, and he feels it with you. He has grieved too.

In the course of Jesus' life on earth, he lost many friends and family to death. Though we are not sure exactly what happened to Jesus' father, Joseph, he may have died, leaving Jesus without an earthly father. Jesus' cousin and close friend, John the Baptist, fell victim to the martyr's sword. When Jesus heard the news about John, he withdrew to grieve privately. Jesus lost one of his own disciples forever when Judas betrayed him and hanged himself. Jesus lost Lazarus, and he wept.

Jesus then died himself, leaving his disciples and friends to grieve over his death. But rather than leave them (and us) with only promises for the future, Jesus comforted them by returning to life. He understood their grief, and he turned it to joy by returning from the dead. His resurrection is a promise to us that we, too, will one day experience the same thing. And when we do, we will see those who have gone before us.

We do not want you to be uninformed, brothers,
concerning those who are asleep, so that you will not
grieve like the rest, who have no hope. Since we believe
that Jesus died and rose again, in the same way God will

bring with Him those who have fallen asleep through Jesus.

1 Thessalonians 4:13–14

The Bible does not tell us that we shouldn't grieve. It encourages us to understand that our grief is not permanent. It is a temporary sadness at a temporary separation. My uncle is not dead. He is alive and well and waiting for his brothers and sisters and nephews and nieces to join him. The same is true of your Christian friends and family members who have passed on. You will see them again. In this certainty we find great hope.

You will not escape grief in this life. When you choose to love someone today, you choose to grieve for him or her tomorrow if death strikes. Grief is a risk you are willing to take.

Grief is not an event. It is a process, like cooking dinner. The food that goes into the oven is unprepared. For a time it endures intense heat and undergoes change. Then the chef removes it and serves it as the main course of his banquet.

You will be unprepared for the grief that strikes you next. And for a time you will endure deep sorrow. Your life will change. But do not lose hope. God has not abandoned you to this pain. You will not grieve forever. Over time he will comfort you and bring you out of your bereavement.

The raising of Lazarus is a taste of things to come. I can only imagine the reactions of Mary and Martha as their four days of grief ended and Lazarus returned to them alive.

Jesus is coming back. In the meanwhile we grieve. But we grieve knowing that when he arrives, he will ignore the lingering stench of death and roll back the stone that separates us from the ones whom we love. And then he will say the words that will reunite us forever. This is the end of our grieving process. This is our hope.

> *I assure you: An hour is coming and is now here,*
> *when the dead will hear the voice of the Son of God,*
> *and those who hear will live.*
>
> John 5:25

Discussion Questions

Describe your thoughts and feelings on death. Who have you lost to the icy sting of death? How has this loss changed your life? How prepared are you to face death? If you knew you only had a month left to live, what would you do differently? If knowing the date of your death would make you live life differently, then are you really living the way you want to now?

Have you felt that God was far away during the times you have grieved for a loved one? Do you really think God doesn't care about what has happened? What do you think God feels when you feel grief?

What passages of Scripture speak to you the most during times of grief? What are the most meaningful words that someone else has said to you in the middle of your grief?

Why is Jesus so qualified to understand your grief and empathize with you? Describe how you think you might feel on the day that Jesus returns and you see those Christians whom you have lost again. What kind of hope does Jesus' impending return give you now?

---

1. Paul J. Achtemeier, *Harper's Bible Dictionary* (San Francisco: Harper and Row Publishers, Inc., 1985).

Giving All You've Got

CHAPTER NINE

I was part of that strange race of people
aptly described as spending their lives
doing things they detest
to make money they don't want
to buy things they don't need
to impress people they dislike.

—EMILE HENRY GAUVREAU

Recently, a friend and coworker walked into my office and placed a wrapped gift on my desk. "Open it," he said. I eyed him suspiciously. My mental check of the calendar could find no reason for this occasion. No birthday. No holiday. Nothing. So why was my friend giving me a gift?

"Open it!" he reiterated. I picked it up, turned it over in my hands, and began to peel away the paper. Inside were two DVD movies, movies that I really liked but had never bought. I sat speechless and looked up at my friend and said, "Why?"

He gave me a reason, but I still don't understand why he took the time to remember that I liked these movies, go to the store, find them, pay for them, wrap them, and bring them to me in the middle of an otherwise grueling day on the job. He really caught me off guard. But he also really made my day.

Tonight as I think about my friend's generosity, I have a sudden flow of memories of recent and similar events. The other day another friend gave me a DVD and a CD, for no reason other than he knew that I would like them both. A month ago my wife left a greeting card on the bathroom counter for me just to say, "I love you." A neighbor I had never met came to my house a few weeks ago and volunteered to fix a problem that he knew I couldn't. My father-in-law keeps my closet freshly stocked with shoes from the department store where he works. The list goes on and on.

I have come to expect gifts on major holidays. And though I enjoy them, their impact on my life fails to compare to the unexpected, undeserved gifts that come in between. I really like getting those.

You would think that if I like getting gifts like this then I would also practice giving them, but I'm afraid I really don't. When I look at my own record of giving, I pale in comparison to others around me. Most of the time my mind is not on giving; it is on getting. I need to get things done and get my fair share and get ahead and get more stuff. Because, as everyone knows, the more you get the happier you are.

Or is this a myth? Do happiness and contentment come from the abundance of our wealth and our possessions? If you can answer this question confidently in the affirmative, then congratulations. I wish you well in your pursuit of the "stuff" that dreams are made of. But if you are more like me and you already know that material things are not the purpose for living, then join me in an honest look at what it means to have the rights of life, liberty, and the pursuit of happiness. Let's rearrange how we plan to live the few precious days we have been given.

Did you notice that? Did you catch the last word in the last sentence of the previous paragraph? Even I didn't catch it until I started writing this one. *Given.* The lives that we live. The days we have. The air we breathe. The freedom to choose our next move. All of these have been *given* to us. We didn't earn them. We didn't invent them. We didn't manufacture them. All we did was take them from the gracious hand of God. He is the reason we live and move and have our being. He is the supplier of life. Everything that we think, do, and say is possible only because God has provided.

> *Every generous act and every perfect gift is from above, coming down from the Father of lights. With Him there is no variation or shadows cast by turning. By His own choice, He gave us birth by the message of truth so that we would be a firstfruits of His creation.*
> *James 1:17–18*

All that we have is a gift from God, and yet our natural inclinations are the exact opposite. We don't want to give. We want to get. We are never satisfied with what we have. We always want more. And we will do whatever it takes to get it.

For a student of the Bible like me, this causes a problem. The Bible says that we are created in the image of God. God's image, his nature, is to give. Man's image is to get. So why is there such a difference between the nature of God and the actions of mankind?

I submit to you that the difference does not really exist. Oh, at first glance it seems to be there. But if you look deep down inside at the core of every human's heart, I think you will find that we do want to give. We do know that it is better to give than to receive. We are far happier living in generosity than voracity.

We just don't know that we know it.

And so we live contrary to our own desires. We take instead of give. And happiness eludes us. We scratch our heads and wonder why. It is not until we see an example—living proof—of what generosity can do that we pause to consider if there really is another way to live.

❧ ❧ ❧

Based on
Matthew 26:6–13;
Mark 14:3–10;
John 12:1–8

Mary anticipated the day of Jesus' arrival with mixed feelings. On the one hand, she could not wait. On the other, she knew that Jesus' time on earth was short. She was one of the few who understood clearly what Jesus was about to go through. In less than one week he would be arrested, beaten, tortured, crucified, and buried. Mary's suburban home was to be Jesus' base as he traveled back and forth to Jerusalem each day. She wanted his final hours to be special. But how? What could she do?

Her sister, Martha, already knew what she would do. She was a culinary queen, and her way of giving to Jesus would be to pre-pare savory meals each day when Jesus returned from Jerusalem. Mary could certainly cook, but it just wasn't her thing. She wanted to do something more. Even Lazarus, Mary's brother, had it easy. All he had to do was show up for dinner each day. The entire coun-tryside came in throngs to see Lazarus, the man whom Jesus had raised from the dead. But Mary felt as if she had nothing. No skills. No fame. Nothing to offer.

Perhaps it was not until the day of Jesus' arrival that it struck her. As she stared out of her window one day, she remembered. She turned and saw it there on the shelf, a sealed alabaster jar of scented oil. It was her only possession of any real value. It came from the Himalayan Mountains in faraway India. In monetary terms it was worth more than one year of an average man's salary. In sentimental terms it was priceless. She had been saving it for a special occasion, perhaps even for her wedding night or an anniver-sary. But now she could think of no reason to save it any longer.

The occasion had come, and its ultimate purpose now seemed perfectly clear to her.

She held it, rotating it in her hands as she had done thousands of times before. This jar was full of more than perfume. It was full of dreams and hope and romance. She treasured it more than any other earthly possession. And that is precisely why she chose to give it away.

"Dinner is ready!" she heard her sister call from the kitchen. The house was full of guests, and Mary did not want to steal the attention away from Martha's feast. So she set the jar down one last time in its place and took her seat at the table.

Mary never heard a word of the conversation over dinner. She ate in silence, almost unable to contain herself. She watched Jesus as he spoke to the other guests. Finally, when everyone seemed to be finished and Martha had removed the last plate from its setting, Mary rose.

She rushed into her room and tried to gain some semblance of composure. She removed the straps that held up her hair, allowing it to cascade past her shoulders and down her back. She sat down for a moment and brushed her hair, rehearsing her next move. Then she turned and picked up the alabaster jar. She held it close, careful not to drop it, and walked back to the dinner table. Jesus was still there—as was most everyone else. She walked over to him and stood.

The conversations around the table began to dissipate in gradual waves as the guests noticed Mary. Her hair was down. Her face, radiant. No one had any doubt something important was about to happen.

Mary knelt down in front of Jesus. With a gentle crack she broke open the neck of the bottle and emptied its contents on Jesus' feet and head. She gave each foot a gentle bath in the perfume, careful not to miss a single spot. She massaged the oil into Jesus' scalp. Then she leaned forward and used her hair to wipe off the excess.

The oil's essence crept through the room and filled the entire house with its aroma. Mary was still kneeling before Jesus when the silence broke. Everyone was amazed at this lavish display. Some of them knew how much this perfume meant to Mary. Some of them discussed the appropriateness of such a scene. One of them spoke aloud.

"Why in the world would you take something worth a year of a man's life and do something so wasteful? We should have sold this and given the money to the poor." It was Judas. Judas didn't care about the poor. All Judas cared about was the amount of money lining his pockets. As treasurer for the disciples, Judas often took a nice percentage for himself. He didn't see Mary's gift. He only saw something that he could have had.

"Judas, leave her alone," Jesus defended. "Mary knows that this perfume is meant to prepare me for burial. The poor will always be available for you to help, Judas. I will not. And because of her gift to me, the whole world will hear her story from now until the end of time." At that moment Judas realized that his dreams of becoming rich off Jesus' fame would never happen. That very evening he went to the religious leaders and made an arrangement to betray Jesus, trading his Master for thirty pieces of silver.

If you stand Mary and Judas side by side, you see two people who knew Jesus well. One of them gave her most prized possession to Jesus in a single act of extravagant love. The other decided that Jesus stood between him and his most prized possession—wealth. One gave. One took. One loved. One betrayed.

The quest for wealth can make us do crazy things. How ironic that most people seek wealth.

What you give is your choice.

No one told Mary that she had to give anything to Jesus. Jesus did not issue a challenge to the dinner guests to see who could produce the most lavish gift. Mary saw Jesus and saw her perfume and couldn't imagine the two apart.

When my son awoke from his afternoon nap, my wife offered him a cup of juice. As he gulped the beverage, Jennifer also gave him a peanut butter cookie. With one hand he continued to drink, and with the other he took the treat. As I am in the habit of doing, I knelt down to Ryan and prodded, "And what do you say?"

I expected him to look at his mother and say, "Thank you." Instead, he looked at me, lifted up the cookie, and said, "Want some?"

I have never asked my son to share his food with me. Yet he chose to take one of his most prized possessions, a cookie, and offer it to his father. My heart melted. I didn't need Ryan's cookie, but I took some of it because he wanted to give it to me.

God does not need your money to feed the poor or build your church a new building or provide for an overseas missionary. He can fund all of that himself in whatever way he sees fit. But he will certainly appreciate it if you choose to give something to any of these causes.

Giving is not a matter of God's need. It is a matter of your willingness. God likes it when you voluntarily give because it communicates that you love and trust him.

> *I want each of you to take plenty of time to think it over, and make up your own mind what [and how] you will give. That will protect you against sob stories and arm-twisting. God loves it when the giver delights in the giving.*
>
> 2 Corinthians 9:7 The Message

Whatever and however you choose to give is up to you. God does not want your gift if you really don't want to give it. He wants cheerful givers more than he wants sizable gifts.

And money isn't the only thing you can give. Mary's choice was using a valuable gift to create a memorable experience. I have a good friend who donates a quilt every year to an auction for the local crisis pregnancy center. A couple I know gave their car to someone who really needed it. My wife is donating her time to help get the preschool ministry of our new church off the ground. A young man I know once gave brand-new tennis shoes to a hitch-hiker who had worn out his own. I have another friend who gave up her place in a long line to an elderly woman.

Let's talk specifics. What opportunities exist in your world for cheerful giving?

Church. I believe that the Bible makes clear that the primary avenue for giving is in your local fellowship. The New Testament Book of Acts, which is a documentary of the formation and ministry of the early church, sets the precedent.

Now the multitude of those who believed were of one heart and soul, and no one said that any of his possessions was his own, but instead they held everything in common. And with great power the apostles were giving testimony to the resurrection of the Lord Jesus, and great grace was on all of them. For there was not a needy person among them, because all those who owned lands or houses sold them, brought the proceeds of the things that were sold, and laid them at the apostles' feet. This was then distributed to each person as anyone had a need.

Acts 4:32–35

There is no church building mentioned in this passage. The church is not a building. It is a group of believers who cheerfully commit to love and provide for one another.

Look around at your fellow church members. How can you be a cheerful giver to them? If you're having trouble, let me give you an example.

My air conditioner went out a few summers ago. In Texas, when an air conditioner goes out in the summer, you either buy a new air conditioner or buy a new house. I couldn't afford either.

Fortunately, I had a friend at church named Scott who knew something about air conditioners. He came to my house and diagnosed the problem. He helped me get a discount on the parts I needed. He helped install them. Before long my house was nice and cool again.

Scott has done the same thing for probably twenty other families. He has an air-conditioning ministry. And he never charges a dime for his services.

Take an inventory of the money, possessions, skills, and time you have. Then match those against the needs of others in your church. Then choose to do what you can. That's all God asks.

People may not understand your choice.

Despite Judas's greed, his statement was still correct. Mary could have sold the perfume and given a large sum of money to help feed the homeless and hungry. Nevertheless, Jesus honored Mary's choice when it didn't make sense to anyone else.

God does not calculate value the same way we do. We analyze the cost-to-benefit ratio. God analyzes the heart.

I recently heard that someone donated a Bible that cost eight-thousand dollars to a church. They are going to display it behind a glass case in a prominent location. It's about three feet wide and four or five feet tall. I have to confess that my first thought was, *What a waste! What good is an eight-thousand dollar Bible? Why not use that money to send kids to camp or buy food for the hungry?*

Then I sat down to write this chapter. My tune changed quickly when I read the words of Judas. First, I cannot judge either the gift or the giver because I know little about either. And second, the gentleman who gave this Bible did so much in the same way that Mary gave her perfume. It is a lavish gift, something that will call attention to God and his Word. God does not see this Bible as money that could have been used more productively. He sees a man who cheerfully gave. I think that's the true spirit of giving.

It really doesn't matter what I think, though. It doesn't matter what anyone thinks. When you feel like expressing your love to God through a gift, do it. Let God be the sole judge of what you do.

You will get back more than you give.

Judas was disappointed and angry at seeing that much money slip through his fingers. In an effort to get some of it back, he sold Jesus for thirty pieces of silver. But that sum did not buy him happiness. It bought him suicide. He felt so guilty later for his betrayal that he hanged himself.

Contrast this with Mary, a simple woman from a small village who would have probably lived and died in obscurity were it not for this event. Jesus promised that her gift would make it into the Bible, and it did. Christians and churches around the world retell the story of Mary and her generous spirit. She attained a fame she could have never bought with money.

Your gifts to God do not go unnoticed. He is a divine accountant. And he promises that whatever you give will return to you in equal or greater degrees.

> *Give, and it will be given to you; a good measure, pressed down, shaken together, and running over will be poured into your lap. For with the measure that you use, it will be measured back to you.*
>
> *Luke 6:38*

In college I once faced what now seems a meager financial crisis. I had thirty dollars to last me through the rest of the month. I decided I would spend it carefully, wringing every last ounce of value from those greenbacks.

That week I ran into a friend who also faced a financial crisis. He and his family were poor and lived a few miles away. He explained that he and his single mom would not make it that month unless extra money came out of nowhere.

I thought about the money in my pocket, and then I thought about my friend. I felt God prompt me to give the thirty dollars away because this young man could use it more than I could. I wrestled with God for some time before I finally decided I could never win a match against the Almighty.

I gave my friend the thirty dollars. His eyes lit up, and he thanked me. He took it home to his mother, and they stretched it much further than I ever would have.

The next day a friend of mine from home called and asked if I could help her father install a disk drive on the family computer. I agreed and stopped by on my way home for the weekend. After I finished the job, I drove home thinking about how I would ever make it one more week without money. I didn't want to ask my parents for help, so I told them nothing.

The next morning I ran into my friend again. She walked over and put something in my hand. "My father wanted you to have this," she said. In my hand was thirty dollars.

God took care of me. He gave me back exactly what I gave to him. And since that time I have discovered that the more I give, the more God gives back to me. He has never let me down. He won't let you down either.

Discussion Questions

You've probably seen generous people on television or from a distance. Who is the most generous person you know? How has his or her generosity changed the way you think about happiness and wealth?

How active is your giving—your unselfish offerings of time, money, effort, etc.? Give specific examples of where you are doing well in these areas. What about areas in which you could improve? Do you ever begrudge the check you write to your church or the time you give to someone in need? What will it take for you to be more cheerful in your giving?

Have you ever misunderstood or critically judged someone else's gift? Have you ever felt misunderstood or critically judged because of your own methods of giving? What is the craziest thing that you sense God calling you to give? Why not go for it?

Can you think of any examples in your life where you gave until it hurt and then later watched how God gave it back? How can you give until it hurts today?

Looking Beyond Yourself

CHAPTER TEN

If you want happiness for an hour—take a nap. If you want happiness for a day—go fishing. If you want happiness for a month—get married. If you want happiness for a year—inherit a fortune. If you want happiness for a lifetime—help someone else.

—CHINESE PROVERB

"Free car wash."

You've seen the signs before. You may have even held one. It's easy to read, but that's not what it says. The words say, "Free car wash." But the meaning is, "Leave a nice donation, please, because we washed your car and surely you wouldn't make us do it for free."

Don't get me wrong. Fundraisers have their place. Car washes can raise funds. And that's what we expect them to be doing when we see a group of people in a storefront parking lot with towels, hoses, and buckets.

Recently my church offered a free car wash in a drugstore parking lot. Only it really was free. No donations accepted. Period.

People were amazed. They kept searching their purses for checkbooks and fishing in pockets for cash. My fellow washers would shake their heads and put up their hands. "No donations."

"But the sign said 'free car wash,'" they would point out. "That means you want donations."

"No—it means 'free,'" we would say. And they tried to ponder this new meaning for the word *free*. We would offer cold drinks—also for free.

I had a good laugh watching everyone's reactions. I talked to a lot of people who wanted to know what the catch was. "No catch," I would say. "God's love is free. So is ours. Have a great day."

A truly free car wash is an oddity in our society. And that's unfortunate. Most people realize that all the other people around them are thinking about themselves—because they, too, are thinking about themselves. It's what people do. It's what we're made to do. Right?

That's what we think most of the time. We think about ourselves. We do things for ourselves. And every now and then, when we find a spare moment or two, we might think about and do something for someone else.

That's why it catches us off guard so much when we see someone living outside this paradigm. We don't understand them. We are suspicious of them. We wonder what makes them tick.

That's what happened at our car wash as we knelt down to clean the dirt that was hiding in the crevices. It's also what happened when God did the same thing.

Based on John 13:1–17

Thirteen men who would change the world now reclined on elbows around the small foot-high table in the second-story guest room. An unlikely lot, these men were no warriors. They were not military strategists or Nobel prize-winning scientists. They were simple and unassuming, largely unknown even in their own country. They were scruffy and disheveled. Their clothes were modest. Their faces, plain.

Oil lamps on the walls provided only modest lighting against the backdrop of early evening. A cool April air circulated through the room between small windows.

Dinner was almost ready. Some men talked to those seated next to them. Some quietly reflected on recent events. One fidgeted nervously. One stood.

Jesus rose from the table, and the disciples gradually fell silent, assuming he would offer the Passover blessing. Instead Jesus walked quietly to the wall behind them and took off his outer clothing, leaving only a one-piece, knee-length undergarment. He knelt to the floor and picked up a towel, wrapping it around his waist. He reached for a water jar and poured its contents into a large, shallow bowl. Then he returned to the table and knelt down again at the feet of one of the disciples.

Some gasped. Others remained motionless and wide-eyed. Peter lurched forward to get up in protest, but his brother Andrew stayed him.

What was about to happen was not so unusual. The disciples had often received such courtesies prior to an evening meal but never by anyone other than a nameless household servant. Like most average people, they normally washed their own feet prior to the evening meal. But to see a king kneeling before his own servants was unprecedented.

Jesus unlaced the sandals of the first disciple, Matthew, and placed them to one side. He cupped his right hand under Matthew's left heel and then dipped it into the basin of water. Jesus gently scrubbed the speechless disciple's foot, careful to get between the toes, and rinsed it. Finally, using one end of the towel hanging around his waist, he patted the foot dry and replaced the sandal. He repeated this procedure for the other foot.

In the meanwhile Jesus made eye contact with Matthew. Here was a tax collector, a man known once for his quest for riches and now known for little else. Matthew had done and said little during the past three years. You might even say he was insignificant. Jesus saw beyond the past and into the future. He saw the man who would someday have his name first in a line of books that would form the New Testament. Matthew's account would be a thorough and spectacular chronicle of all that Jesus had done in his public ministry. His comprehensive volume would be instrumental in leading many others to trust in Jesus as the Son of God, the same man who now relaced the second sandal and smiled at Matthew as he moved to the next man.

James was next. Some called him James the Lesser, to distinguish him from John's brother. Not a single word or action is attributed to this James during his travels with Jesus. Jesus knew, though, that James would one day die a martyr's death in service to him.

Now to Thomas, later nicknamed "Doubting Thomas." In the three moments mentioned about him in the Bible, Thomas is questioning, doubting, and battling depression. His nature is to be pessimistic. In a few days Thomas would refuse to accept the possibility that Jesus had risen from the dead until he saw him with his own eyes. Still Jesus tenderly cleansed the feet of this hesitant disciple, knowing that one day Thomas's doubts would turn into such a great faith that he would willingly die at the hands of an angry pagan's spear.

Simon the Zealot, with fire still bright in his eyes, fidgeted as Jesus washed his feet. Simon was once affiliated with a political extremist group seeking to overthrow the Roman government by force. His feet, perhaps still itching to march into war, now sat peaceful and clean by the hands of God. Those same feet that once chose violence would one day succumb to it as a nail pierced them both in crucifixion.

Next is Nathanael, also known as Bartholomew. Prideful skepticism and political ambition marked his first encounter and only recorded conversation with Jesus. Jesus saw past Nathanael's critical eye into a heart that was quick to pledge him eternal allegiance. He would later carefully translate his friend Matthew's Gospel into other languages so that other skeptics could read the story of Jesus.

Philip was next. He introduced Nathanael to Jesus. Philip believed what he saw with his eyes and distrusted anything he could not. He now saw his Lord removing crust from between his toes, and it changed his life forever. Less than twenty years from now, Philip would be beaten and crucified for his role in helping others see Jesus.

Judas, also known as Thaddaeus, had the misfortune of sharing the same name as the traitor, Judas Iscariot. His only recorded word to Jesus is "Why?" Why are you doing things this way, God? He undoubtedly wanted to know why Jesus now rinsed away the dust of his travels. Jesus knew that Judas would understand why his role in leading hundreds of people to Jesus would earn him a martyr's death on a cross.

Judas Iscariot could not look Jesus in the eyes, but Jesus did not turn away or refrain from washing the feet of this thief and betrayer. Judas often stole money from the disciples' treasury and feigned goodwill when pleading to others for more money to support the group. Even now, as Jesus dried the soles of his feet, Judas was counting the purse he would soon receive for getting Jesus arrested. Jesus could already taste the sting of Judas's kiss of betrayal in the garden just a few hours away. How ironic that the thirty pieces of silver Judas would receive for turning Jesus in equaled the current market value of a household slave, a part Jesus now played. Jesus relaced these shoes and looked with love into the eyes of the man who would betray him and then commit suicide by this time tomorrow.

Andrew, a faithful follower, was always bringing someone to Jesus. He brought his brother Peter to Jesus. He brought the young boy with five loaves of bread and two fish to Jesus before the miraculous feeding of the five thousand. Andrew brought a group of curious Greek men to Jesus in order to have some of their tough questions answered. Jesus caressed the feet he knew would one day be bound with ropes on an X-shaped cross, where Andrew would suffer for three full days before dying. During those painful hours Andrew would bring hundreds of people to Jesus by sharing his faith with all who came to witness his execution.

James, the brother of John, a simple fisherman, had tremendous desire for fame and power. He demanded with his brother, John, to be honored in heaven as the greatest humans ever to live. He wanted to call down fire to destroy a handful of people who once stood in Jesus' way. Part of Jesus' inner circle, he witnessed more of Jesus' miracles than most of the other disciples. John's feet often ran too quickly and in the wrong direction, but Jesus tamed them with his gentle discipline and redirection. James would one day be first, the first disciple of Jesus to be killed for his faith. On the day of his execution, he walked slowly but unwaveringly toward the swordsman.

John came to one conclusion after his travels with the Son of God—that Jesus loved him. He referred to himself "as the one Jesus loved" in the book he would write to share Jesus with the world. Jesus loved him so much that he would soon place his aging mother in John's care. He, too, sought the power and fame of his brother, James. He later was exiled to a remote island where he wrote the Book of Revelation and died a natural death at the approximate age of one hundred.

Jesus nicknamed Peter, "The Rock." Some have nicknamed him, "The Mouth." Peter was the only one to break the sacred silence of this moment with meaningless words. Peter's mouth had *already, and would continue, to get him into much trouble. The same mouth that openly declared Jesus as the Son of God would also angrily oppose Jesus in his mission to die on the cross. In a few moments Peter would swear he would die for Jesus. Before sunrise he would swear with curses that he had never met Jesus. Not far behind Peter's big mouth was his impetuous and often misdirected zeal. He once jumped out of a boat to walk with Jesus on the water, only to sink in his faithlessness. In a few hours he would draw a sword and sever the ear (though his intent was likely for the whole head) of someone trying to arrest Jesus. But that same body would one day stand a few feet away, in the doorway to this room, and use that same mouth to preach a rousing sermon that would convince more than five thousand people to dedicate their lives to Jesus forever. Jesus dried Peter's feet knowing that they would one day lead the disciples forward. They would also lead him out to be crucified upside down as his final act of faith.*

Jesus stood and stretched his legs, returning the water and towel to its place. He dressed himself properly and returned to the table to join his friends. He looked at each of them one last time. He thought, Here are the men who will carry on my mission. Here are the men who will change the world. *And yet, here are the men who would fall asleep tonight when Jesus asked them to pray with him. These same feet, now clean, would be kicking up a cloud of dust as they ran away and abandoned Jesus during the hour he needed them most.*

Jesus washed the feet of all twelve of his disciples regardless of their past, present, and future. Why? Why would he do this? The Bible tells us there are two reasons. First, Jesus loved each of these men with all of his heart. Jesus washed their feet to show them the full extent of his love (see John 13:1). Second, Jesus did it to give these men an example to follow. Jesus didn't want that night to be a one-time event. His actions were a silent sermon on how to treat the people that God places in our lives. This message is given primarily in the context of how to treat your fellow believers—those specifically within your church family.

The disciples formed the first church. They walked with and learned about Jesus together. They depended on one another and functioned as a unit. And their mission was to share Jesus, through words and actions, with the rest of the world. They are a microcosmic depiction of the church today—whether large or small, city or country, homeland or foreign, yours or mine.

It should come as no surprise, then, when we look at the church as a whole or in our own local body, that we find that both are far from perfect. If you are involved in a church now, you know from an insider's perspective just how true this is. You see character flaws, power plays, divisive issues, financial improprieties, and a multiplicity of hotly contested opinions on the "right" methods to use in ministry and worship. We rub shoulders weekly with some we love, a few that we dislike, and many that we simply don't know.

Beyond our own walls are other Christian churches within the community. Some do things like we do. Many do not. Some are sisters in denominational affiliation. Others are distant cousins. Some raise hands. Some fold them. Yours has great music. The one down the street uses instruments that make you shiver. All of them have problems, including yours.

With such diversity and dysfunction comes the natural tendency to like those like you and do any number of things to those who are not—dislike, avoid, ignore, judge, fight, or even hate.

In the midst of this troubled age of the church, God yearns for something more. He longs for us to come together in spite of our differences. He longs for unity among his followers. His demonstration of love to such a diverse group around the table at the Last

Supper is not the only indication of this desire. Later this same evening Jesus gives us three more glimpses into the power and importance of unity in his family of believers.

One new command.

As Jesus concluded his earthly ministry on the eve of his crucifixion, he began to transfer the responsibility of his mission to his disciples. In so doing he thought it wise to leave his disciples with one new command. Just one. His entire ministry on earth boiled down to a simple sentence. You can imagine the importance of this request.

> *I give you a new commandment: that you love one another. Just as I have loved you, you should also love one another.*
>
> *John 13:34*

The disciples felt their feet still tingling from their unexpected bath when they heard Jesus share these words. I think they heard him loud and clear.

One proof for the existence of God.

Those outside the church often say that if they had proof that God existed they would choose to believe in and follow him. Those of us inside the church often try to use our brains to concoct foolproof arguments to support the claim that Jesus is the Son of God. That proof exists, but we often hide it behind our own stained glass and stained records. Jesus has already told us what evidence will convince the world of his reality and his love.

> *By this all people will know that you are My disci-*
> *ples, if you have love one for another.*
>
> *John 13:35*

Scientific evidence and impregnable theological arguments are not what will convince those around you that Jesus is for real. What will convince them are the actions that back up your words. Actions that include sacrificial care and concern for the people around you. There is no greater impact than true love lived out as an example for others to see.

One prayer for the future church.

Just before Jesus was arrested, he prayed for his disciples. He also whispered a lone prayer for his future disciples, the church today. In that prayer, Jesus made one request.

> *I pray not only for these, but also for those who*
> *believe in Me through their message. May they all be*
> *one, just as You, Father, are in Me and I am in You. May*
> *they also be one in Us, so that the world may believe*
> *You sent me.*
>
> *John 17:20–21*

Strange, isn't it? Jesus did not ask for packed pews. He did not request multimillion-dollar facilities, powerful sermons, and state-of-the-art music ministries. He did not pray for big budgets and big productions. He asked for one thing: unity. Jesus knows that unity is the key to success in the church.

Keep in mind that unity does not mean uniformity. We do not have to be the same. God has deliberately designed us to be different. That disparate group of disciples still managed to complete their mission and transform the world with the message of Jesus' love and forgiveness. We can do the same but only if we consciously choose to love those who are different from us.

One new command. One proof for God. One prayer for the church. We can no longer ignore the critical importance of unity and love within our churches. The health and success of our mission is at stake. When the unchurched world stops at an intersection and sees four churches, they ask, "Why? If there is only one God, then why are there four churches?" When denominational disputes make the evening news, we are not helping our cause.

The solution lies in godly love. Love those who are right and love those who are wrong. Love those who are like you and those who are not. Love the rich and the poor, the skinny and the fat, the tall and the short, the intelligent and the ignorant. Love your enemies and love your friends. Love the attractive and the annoying. Love.

It's not easy. I know. Loving people who are different takes work. And the amount of work to be done is always directly proportional to the number of excuses we devise to dismiss ourselves from the responsibility. Hundreds of such pretexts exist, but for brevity's sake here I present only three popular reasons we use to sidestep our duty to love those around us.

It's not my job.

Can you say *compartmentalization*? I can already see the pie chart that represents your life because it looks a lot like mine. This slice is devoted to a full-time job—including the time you think about it, drive to and from it, or work at it from outside the office. Over here is parenting and family time. Church time gets a sliver. Then there are chores and errands, with a little bit left for recreation and a few other things. You've got it all figured out.

So when you're in "commute time" and you pass the stranded motorist, your pie chart doesn't have a predesignated slice for "helping out on the highway." Surely the city or county police will be by any minute to assist this person. It's not your job; you're late for dinner. Better keep moving.

Many churches, including my own, are meeting in temporary facilities—school cafeterias or gymnasiums, college auditoriums, or empty storefronts. To carry out a single service, these churches need an army of volunteers to set up chairs, configure sound equipment, create children's ministry areas, serve breakfast, work at the welcome center for guests, volunteer to teach, and a host of other things. And that's just on Sunday morning. Sunday afternoon they have to do the reverse. Without a doubt these churches would not survive unless everyone pitched in to do anything that needs to be done. They survive and succeed because people see a need and donate their time. It's that simple.

It was not Jesus' job to wash the disciples' feet. This duty belonged to the obsequious, not the Omniscient. The disciples could have done it themselves. Jesus could have paid or arranged for someone to do this service for him, but it wouldn't have been the same. He *wanted* to do this himself.

I had this same mind-set one night as I drove back to Dallas from Houston after Christmas. Outside it was dark, cold, and rainy. Inside I turned up the heater to keep my family nice and toasty. We were about halfway home when I saw headlights flashing in the wide median up ahead. I immediately assumed it was a state trooper on the prowl. I checked my speed. OK, safe. In the dark and at 65 mph it was hard to determine, but it appeared that a car was stranded and trying to signal for help.

I flew right by, thinking that either my assessment was wrong or that, if I was right, someone else would surely stop to help out, someone without a wife and child and more than a hundred miles to go. Then I realized that every other driver out there was probably thinking the same thing. Who knows how long this car had been there? I looked at my wife and said, "We've got to turn around." She didn't argue.

It took awhile to find another exit, but we made a U-turn and made our way back to the car, still there and obviously trapped. I got out of my car with my cell phone and walked through fifty yards of mud. When I arrived at the car, I found a young lady traveling by herself. Her car had spun off the road and into the median, leaving her so deep in the mud that she could not open either car door to get out. She had been there for an hour trying to signal for help with her headlights. Her engine had stalled, and she was beginning to get cold. She had no phone and no idea what to do next. I called the state police and requested a tow truck. She made a quick call to a friend.

That's all it took. A few minutes of my time and a little mud on my shoes and she would be home—perhaps late but definitely safe. If I had kept driving, as I almost did, who knows how long she might have been out there?

I don't know about you, but I am pleasantly surprised when someone chooses to do something good for me—something not in his or her job description. It gets my attention. It causes me to pause and take note. It makes me want to return the favor.

This kind of giving does much more. Spontaneous and selfless acts of compassion and service reveal the character and presence of God. It is not God's job to love us, but he does. And when you, in turn, imitate God in this regard, the recipients of your kindness will see God and his love.

They don't deserve it.

The men seated around the table at the Last Supper certainly did not deserve the kind favor of clean feet. One of them was an unbeliever, a fraud, and a thief. All of them had severe weaknesses in character and faith. Still, Jesus humbly knelt before them and served.

We too often justify our lack of service to others by eliminating them in the qualifying rounds with cursory judgment. The bum on the street corner holding the sign is probably an alcoholic, so lock your doors, roll up your windows, and pretend to be looking at something else. The pregnant teenager sitting on the back row by herself deserves to be shunned; look at what she's done to herself. Those people who sit on the "other side of the church" are stirring trouble, so leave them out of your prayers.

What would Jesus do if he walked into your church and saw these people in attendance? Would he steer clear of them because of their failures? No. In fact, he would do just the opposite. These would be the people he sought to be nearest because they are the ones who need him most right now.

Imagine if your bank deducted money from your account every time you committed a sin. How long would you be able to survive? Or what if your car refused to start every time your attitude wasn't just right? Most of us would starve to death if the refrigerator and pantry closed their doors in protest of our behavior.

Jesus' entire life was a continuous strand of grace offered to those who did not deserve it. Jesus knew that Judas would betray him, but he did not treat him any different from the other disciples.

Therefore, anyone of you who judges is without excuse. For when you judge another, you condemn yourself, since you, the judge, do the same things. We know that God's judgment on those who do such things is based on the truth. Do you really think—anyone of

you who judges those who do such things yet do the
same—that you will escape God's judgment? Or do you
despise the riches of His kindness, restraint, and
patience, not recognizing that God's kindness is
intended to lead you to repentance?

Romans 2:1–4

Kindness, not judgment, is what we need to right the wrongs
in our churches and the people who populate them.

I won't get anything in return.

Reciprocity is a healthy recipe for relationships. I show you
kindness in the subconscious hope that you will do the same for
me. Marriages and friendships often suffer greatly when one gives
more than the other does. Getting something back is important
because it helps us to know that our efforts have not been in vain.

However, the overarching philosophy of Western individual-
ism has led us to such a strict observance of this principle that a
universal stalemate exists; everyone is waiting for everyone else to
do "his part." We consciously or subconsciously keep a record
of who owes whom, or we size up the intended recipient of our
service to determine the potential reward. If we don't like the
odds, we pass.

If Jesus were expecting something in return from the men he
served on the evening of the Last Supper, he should have thrown in
the towel before he ever tied it around his waist. Betrayal, denial,
suicide, sleepy disregard, confusion, broken promises, attempted
murder, and brisk retreat would be all Jesus would get out of these
men tonight. Not only would the disciples fail to reciprocate, but
they would also abandon Jesus altogether.

As we carry out the mission that Jesus has given to us between now and the time he returns, our principal concern cannot be "what's in it for me." Instead, it must be "I'm in it for them."

> *If then there is any encouragement in Christ,*
> *if any consolation of love,*
> *if any fellowship with the Spirit,*
> *if any affection and mercy,*
> *fulfill my joy by thinking the same way,*
> *having the same love,*
> *sharing the same feelings,*
> *focusing on one goal.*
> *Do nothing out of rivalry or conceit,*
> *but in humility consider others as more important*
>   *than yourselves.*
> *Everyone should look out not only for his own*
>   *interests,*
> *but also for the interests of others.*
>
> *Make your own attitude that of Christ Jesus,*
> *who, existing in the form of God,*
> *did not consider equality with God*
> *as something to be used for His own advantage.*
> *Instead He emptied Himself*
> *by assuming the form of a slave,*
> *taking on the likeness of men.*
> *And when He had come as a man in His eternal*
>   *form,*
> *He humbled Himself*
> *by becoming obedient to the point of death—*
> *even to death on a cross.*
>
> *Philippians 2:1–8*

When we do not give because we do not expect to get anything in return, we live a life unlike that of Jesus. When we show kindness, we are following his example.

The culture we live in lies entrenched in a class structure that draws lines between the entitled and unentitled on a variety of fronts. Our free-market economy dictates that we must work to make money and that we must obtain goods and services with that money. You don't walk into a home improvement store and walk out with a new refrigerator without first paying for it. No business would survive without an expected exchange, would it?

Last night I met my wife at the mall with a few other couples. The men pushed the children around in strollers and the women darted in and out of stores in search of bargains. All in all it was a great evening until I returned to my car. I put the key in the ignition and turned it. Silence. Not even a click. Then I noticed that the switch for the headlights was on. My battery was dead. The mall was closed. What was I going to do?

I tracked down mall security and asked if they had jumper cables. "No, but here's the card of a local service man." I reluctantly took the card and thought that I was about to be out $50 or more just to get a jump start. I keyed in the number on my cell phone and explained my plight to the man who answered.

"Sure, I can come out and jump your car for you. I won't charge you anything. I just work for tips."

I hung up the phone in disbelief. Free roadside assistance? Surely he must be joking. A few minutes later he arrived, started my car, and would have left if I hadn't stopped him to give him all the cash I had, which still wasn't enough in my opinion. He said a cheerful "thanks" and drove on.

I did not deserve this man's time on Friday evening, but he gave it to me anyway. He risked leaving without a single dime. He walked away with more than a small tip. He walked away with my full loyalty for future business. His card will never leave my pocket. And I will tell others about him. And I will send him a check on Monday to cover the difference in what I lacked last night—not because he asked me to but because he made me want to pay him more.

That's the kind of effect Jesus had on his disciples. That's the effect the church should, and can, have on the world. We ought to be so caring and so giving that those outside the church are shocked into wanting to know more about us. Right now many churches are pursuing growth by trying to improve "the show" that occurs once a week on the inside. Why not instead work together in unity to throw everything we have into meeting the needs of the people in our community who are on the outside of the building? When they see us give expecting nothing in return, we will find that the walls can no longer contain those wanting to come inside and find the source for our love— God himself.

Discussion Questions

One new command. One proof for God's existence. One prayer for the church. How does Jesus' emphasis on loving and serving others during the final night of his life help you better understand his purpose for coming to earth? How does it help you better understand your purpose for coming to earth?

What opportunities for helping others did you avoid this week because they were "not your job?" What opportunities have you taken advantage of?

Have you overlooked an opportunity to help someone out because you thought they didn't deserve your service? Why? What will it take for you to look past other people's faults in order to be kind to them?

Look back over your week. How have you avoided helping someone because you were afraid you would never see the favor returned? Do you ever find yourself in a stalemate relationship with someone because both of you are waiting on the other to act first? What will it take for you to make the first move?

A Prescription
for Pain

CHAPTER ELEVEN

*The human spirit will not even begin to try to surrender self-will
as long as all seems to be well with it. Now error and sin both
have this property, that the deeper they are the less their victim
suspects their existence. Pain is unmasked, unmistakable evil;
every man knows that something is wrong when he is being hurt.*

—C. S. LEWIS

Both you and I spend a substantial part of our lives enduring
some form of suffering, whether physical or emotional or a combination of both. Much of the pain we experience can be directly attributed to someone else—from a lone individual to an entire army. Other
types of pain come from natural causes, such as weather-related dis-
asters, accidents, disease, and old age. These two distinct forms of suffering deserve different handling, and in this chapter I would like to
focus only on the former. When we are hurt because of someone else's
negligence or malice, we want to do something about it.

The instinctive solution is to strike back in vengeance.
Vengeance can mean returning the same blow, justifying ourselves
with the Old Testament mandate of "an eye for an eye." It can
mean litigation. Or it can mean concocting a whole new realm of
pain for our malefactor in a never-ending battle of one-upmanship.

And even if we are kind enough to choose none of the above, we still have not resolved the issue. Often our retreat is filled with a brooding hatred as we nourish the grudge by repeatedly recalling the offense. At the very least, we are left to lick our wounds in solitude or perhaps in the comfort of a sympathetic ear.

But are these our only solutions? Where is the closure? The justice? What is the purpose of this pain? What do we need to *do* when we suffer at the hands of someone else? We find the answer to this question in observing what Jesus did when he faced the same plight.

Jesus stood. It was nearing midnight. All was quiet. His disciples were scattered and asleep among the olive trees in the garden. The torches of his approaching accusers were just now visible across the

> Based on
> Matthew 27;
> Mark 15; Luke 23;
> John 19

valley as they left Jerusalem in search of their prey. They would be here in minutes.

He begged his Father three times for another way, but he knew now that there was none. He trembled in the breeze, soaked in a bloody perspiration, the result of a spectacular battle between flesh and spirit that became so intense that the capillaries in his skin burst and mixed with his sweat.

Determined to complete the challenge ahead of him, Jesus woke his disciples. They had barely rubbed the sleep from their eyes when a small army of Roman soldiers and Jewish religious officials arrived. Leading them was Judas, a trusted friend. Judas walked over to Jesus and kissed him in mockery as a sign to the soldiers that this was the man to arrest and take away.

Only eleven disciples remained to stand by Jesus as they began to bind Jesus' arms with rope. Before they could finish, one of those eleven, Peter, reacted in anger and unsheathed his sword. He lunged forward and swung, striking the head of the high priest's servant and severing his right ear. Instantly Roman guards stepped forward to kill Peter on the spot, but Jesus intervened. "Stop!" he said. "If you live by the sword, you will surely die by it as well." Then, leaning over the injured and bleeding man, Jesus touched his ear and healed it.

For a moment, no one moved. Then the high priest shouted, "Enough! Let us do what we came here to do and take this criminal away." The soldiers hesitated but finally tied Jesus' arms behind him. The disciples fled in fear, and Jesus disappeared into the night, alone and at the mercy of his captors.

All night long Jesus stood before an illegal jury of so-called religious men who jeered him and prodded him to answer their questions. They would not rest until they could get Jesus to say something incriminating in order to have a basis for taking their case to the Roman governor, Pilate. Despite their repeated attempts at various venues during the course of the night, they failed.

Finally, the high priest leaned forward and asked Jesus plainly, "Are you the Messiah? Tell me. Answer me!" Jesus lifted his eyes and said quietly, "Yes. I am. And though you see me now as a man, you will see me for who I am when I return." The high priest and his associates needed no more hearing. They had their answer. They took him to Pilate at first daylight and demanded a hearing.

Legally speaking, Pilate could find no basis to execute Jesus. The testimony of his accusers was obviously inconsistent. Jesus offered no defense and obviously posed no threat. His so-called crimes were only religious in nature. Pilate addressed the crowd and stated his intentions to release Jesus. But the religious officials incited the people to demand blood. The mob screamed, "Crucify him!"

Pilate hesitated, knowing full well that his authority was being challenged by the religious right wing. In an attempt to appease everyone, he ordered that Jesus be flogged and brought back to the court.

Jesus' hands were tied to a vertical pole in the courtyard to prevent him from moving. His clothing was removed. With a cat-o'-nine-tails two soldiers struck him mercilessly on his bare back. Bone fragments, metal pellets, and sharp rocks that were threaded cruelly into the nine leather tails of the whip tore open his skin and exposed muscle and tissue. Over and over again they struck him, each lash more horrific than its predecessor. Jesus slumped in agony.

The soldiers untied him and threw him to the ground. They kicked him. They spit on him. They plucked the hair from his beard. They draped his bleeding back with a purple robe and knelt before him in ridicule, calling him their King. They blindfolded him and punched him in the face. They made a crown of thorns and smashed it onto his head. And then they brought him back to Pilate in this condition.

Pilate presented Jesus to the crowd in this pitiful condition, convinced that the people would have mercy on the prisoner. But instead, they shouted even louder for nothing less than execution on the cross.

Pilate gave in to the crowd's demands and ordered that Jesus be led away to be crucified. A heavy, wooden cross was strapped to Jesus' back. Soldiers drove him along with two other criminals down a pathway known as the Way of Suffering, or the Via Dolorosa. He endured the relentless pace and the gauntlet of insults until he could go no farther. His strength failed. He stumbled. He fell. He lay face down in the dirt. He could not go on. The weight of his cross was too much. Despite the threats of the soldier behind him, he did not move. Twenty-four hours ago Jesus had stood on his own two feet and held the crowds in the palm of his hands. Now he lay broken and bleeding on the road, and not one person offered assistance.

The soldier responsible for Jesus did not wish for it to appear that he had lost control of the situation, so he drew his sword and pointed it at an approaching traveler named Simon. "You. Pick up this cross and carry it for him." Simon reluctantly obliged. The soldier forced Jesus back to his feet, and the morbid parade continued up the hill known to locals as The Skull.

On reaching the peak, the soldiers grabbed the cross from Simon and threw it on the ground. Then they stripped Jesus of his clothes, reopening the wounds on his back, and threw him onto the cross. One soldier stood on his hand while another stood on his arm. A third centered the tip of a long carpenter's nail over Jesus' wrist. In a few swift strokes the nail tore through flesh, tendons, and bones before finally biting wood. The soldiers repeated this procedure with the other hand. Finally, they moved to his feet. Bending his knees and holding his feet down firmly, one on top of the other, a final nail ripped through them and held them to the cross.

Then the soldiers stood and lifted the cross until it stood almost vertical. They dragged its base to a nearby hole that would serve as its stand. Then they slid it into the hole. The cross fell with a violent jerk, jarring Jesus' already broken body in astonishing pain.

Jesus hung on the cross for approximately six hours, shifting his body in futile efforts to relieve the suffering. At times he would place the weight of his body on the nail in his feet, giving him the ability to breathe. But when his legs cramped and his feet could take the anguish no longer, he would shift the weight to the nails in his wrists. This would stretch his arms beyond their normal length and dislocate the joints in his shoulders and elbows. This position paralyzed the muscles required for breathing outward, so while Jesus could inhale, he could not exhale. This forced him to repeat the procedure all over again by pushing up in an attempt to take another breath. During this time, his blood continued to drain from his body and the chill of death slowly began to take over.

Can you imagine anything more cruel? More painful? And yet, during Jesus' six-hour ordeal of torture on the cross, he did not complain. He was predominantly silent. He spoke only seven times. And yet in his final words from the cross, we find the answer to how we should respond when we suffer pain. I would like to examine each of Jesus' statements in order and illustrate how his immortal words have become our prescription for handling pain and suffering.

Forgive

Jesus said, "Father, forgive them, because they do not know what they are doing."

Luke 23:34

Whom did Jesus forgive from the cross? Jesus forgave Pilate for executing the order for his crucifixion, even though he claimed no responsibility. Jesus forgave the Roman guards for beating him, mocking him, nailing his hands and feet to a cross, and gambling for his clothes as he watched. Jesus forgave the priests who arrested him in the middle of the night, convicted him of false charges during an illegal trial, and handed him over to be crucified. Jesus forgave his disciples for running away at the first sign of trouble. Jesus forgave Peter for publicly denying him three times.

But more than the variety and number of people that Jesus forgave, there is the matter of how he forgave. In this climactic moment Jesus demonstrated that we have no grounds for with-holding forgiveness in any instance. Every possible argument we might have is crushed by the weight of Jesus' grace. Even during his most difficult trial, he sought complete absolution for his malefactors.

But I don't want to forgive. My human nature comes up with many reasons to justify my grudge. For example, when I am hurt by someone else, I often rank the offense into one of several categories of degree. There are petty offenses, such as forgetting to pay me back the fifty cents a coworker borrowed for the vending machine yesterday. Minor offenses include such things as a disregard for punctuality, being cranky in my presence, and not tipping a waiter enough. Between the minor and major offenses lie infractions such as hurting my feelings, driving erratically, or performing a hit-and-run on my mailbox. Finally, the major category is reserved only for the most heinous of crimes, things I would rather not mention.

Jesus' situation obviously qualifies for the worst possible classification. He was betrayed by a friend, abandoned by his team, tried illegally, and murdered by the people he created. He has every right to withhold forgiveness and hold each person involved accountable for his or her part in this tragedy. Instead Jesus is quick to ask for forgiveness.

The baseline that we use to determine whether to offer forgiveness is not the degree of the transgression. It is the example Jesus set on the cross. The reason Jesus went to the cross was to provide forgiveness, so he could not withhold it from those who placed him there.

A second reason we do not think of forgiveness in our pain is that we expect the party responsible for our plight to take the first step. "I will be happy to forgive her if she apologizes." This is a reasonable request, and we certainly cannot deny that it makes reparations easier. But what if you never see an expression of regret from the person who has harmed you? What should your next move be?

You could wait it out. You could demand an apology. You could allow your anger to grow deeper and stronger. Or you could surprise everyone by doing what Jesus did and forgive without the benefit of an admission of guilt.

I will admit this concept goes against the grain. It doesn't even appear at first glance to be logical. I would think that if I were too quick to forgive, then I would invite even more harm. I risk becoming nothing more than a punching bag.

But think about it. When your opponent straps on the gloves and throws the first punch, he expects you to fight back. He may even want you to fight back. The last thing he expects is forgiveness and kindness. He will not know what to do when you give him grace instead of a growl.

King Solomon, the wisest man who ever lived, believed in and recorded this principle in the Old Testament.

> If your enemy is hungry, give him food to eat;
> if he is thirsty, give him water to drink.
> In doing this, you will heap burning coals on his
>   head,
> and the LORD will reward you.
>
> *Proverbs 25:21–22*

In other words, if you *really* want to get back at your enemy, forgive him. Pile on the grace because he will not know what to do with it.

James, the brother of John and one of the twelve apostles of Jesus, was beheaded for his faith. Tradition says that, just like Jesus, James was falsely accused and sentenced to death. On the day of his execution, one of his accusers chose to walk with James and taunt him—not an uncommon practice. The accuser expected to see James react in hate and fear. But James remained calm and forgave his adversary. His confidence was so bold and his grace so amazing that the accuser came to the conclusion that James believed in something real. The man became a Christian on the spot and earned himself a martyr's death alongside James.

The power of grace is limitless, and we do not take advantage of it enough. Every time you have the opportunity to hate and you choose instead to forgive, those around you will recognize the source of that grace. They, too, will be drawn to Jesus.

Focus on the needs of others.

When Jesus saw His mother
and the disciple He loved standing there,
He said to His mother, "Woman, here is your son."
Then He said to the disciple, "Here is your mother."
And from that hour the disciple took her into his
home.

John 19:26–27

Ludwig van Beethoven composed some of the most beautiful music the world will ever know. Even after he became completely deaf, he was able to weave together spectacular melodies and harmonies. He was often frustrated, however, at attempts to talk with friends without being able to listen to them and talk back. Often he would retreat to himself rather than strain to be part of a normal conversation.

Once a close friend of Beethoven's was grieving over the death of a son. When Beethoven heard the news, he agonized over how to comfort his friend. He wanted to say the right words, but he did not know how. Beethoven went to his friend, still wondering what he could possibly say or do. When he arrived at the home, he noticed the piano in the room where his friend sat in sadness. Without a single word Beethoven walked over to the piano, sat down, and began to play as he had never played before. His fingers danced across the keys for some time, flooding the room with soothing music. When he finished, he got up from the piano bench and left. Later, his friend commented to others that he had been comforted more by Beethoven's visit than any other.[1]

When you experience pain, your thoughts are turned inward. You think about the pain and how intense it is and when it will go away and why it had to happen in the first place and who is to blame and what the purpose of it might be. It's easy to forget about the people in your life who still need you.

I am dumbfounded that Jesus had the presence of mind on the cross to see his mother and recognize her anguish. Rather than ask for her pity and her prayers, Jesus reached out to her and provided for her future. He respected and honored her by giving her over to the care of one of his closest disciples.

My lower back hurts from a recent injury. My shoulder blade, knee, and ankle ache from the racquetball game I played this afternoon during a work break. Oh, and did I mention that I have a splitting headache? Surely it is God's irony that I reached this place in the book on the same day that I am plagued by so many ailments. Right now I am tempted to think only of myself. But in just a little while my wife will return home from a Tupperware party. I have two choices when she walks in the door. I can complain about how I feel and wallow in self-pity. Or I can sit down with her, look her in the eye, and ask her to tell me about her evening, nodding approvingly at anything she happened to buy. Which do you think she would prefer? Which would you prefer? The choice is mine, and though I feel like doing the first, I think I will opt for the long-term rewards of the second.

Thinking of others instead of yourself, even when you are suffering, is the right thing to do. And that's precisely why you and I do not want to do it—because it is the right thing to do. We associate doing things right with duty and effort, and our pain makes us want to lie down and do neither. What we really want is freedom from this struggle and attention and comfort from others.

What I am suggesting is that by taking the time to focus on the needs of those around you, you will not only be doing the right thing, you will actually be accomplishing your goals. If you're thinking about and helping someone else, you won't have time to concentrate on yourself and your problem. You will have an interlude of relief. And at the same time, the people you care for will be so amazed by your selflessness that they will *want* to comfort you and take care of you. You will, in effect, get what you want by doing what you don't want.

Don't forget your ministry.

> One of the criminals hanging there began to yell
> insults at Him:
> "Aren't You the Messiah? Save Yourself and us!"
> But the other answered, rebuking him: "Don't you
> even fear God,
> since you are undergoing the same punishment?
> We are punished justly, because we're getting back
> what we deserve for the things we did,
> but this man has done nothing wrong."
> Then he said, "Jesus, remember me when You come
> into Your kingdom!"
> And He said to him, "I assure you: Today you will
> be with Me in paradise."
> *Luke 23:39–43*

Luke's account of the crucifixion says that one thief mocked Jesus and the other made a deathbed confession and became a Christian. The Gospel of Mark says that both thieves taunted him (see Mark 15:32). Which version of the story is correct? Have we found a contradiction in the Bible?

Both Luke and Mark are accurate. Mark's snapshot of this scene simply takes place a little earlier than Luke's does. At the beginning of the crucifixion, both thieves did deride Jesus along with the crowd. The fresh sting of the nails in their wrists and feet brought out the worst. They were angry and spiteful, and nothing good could come out of their mouths.

As time passed, however, the loss of blood and reality of impending death began to weigh heavily on one of the thieves' minds. He grew quiet and began to observe how Jesus acted on the cross. He was amazed that Jesus did not retaliate when insulted. His ears struggled to believe what they heard when Jesus said, "Father, forgive them." He watched in awe as Jesus reached out to his own mother to provide for her. And somewhere in the final hours of his life, this pickpocket had a change of heart. Swept away with the reality and guilt of the charges that earned him an execution, he became acutely aware of the innocence of Jesus. He began to believe the stories he had heard about Jesus. He began to trust this man who died alongside him.

On the other side of Jesus, his former partner in crime continued to bellow his venomous rant. And though once he, too, had participated, the repentant thief could take it no longer. With one of the few short breaths remaining in him, he shouted back in opposition. He whispered to Jesus to allow him into the kingdom of God. Jesus raised his head and looked into his eyes. And in that moment he did not see a thief. He saw a man in need of a Savior.

What caused this hard-core criminal to turn soft? It was how Jesus handled pain.

One of the reasons you and I still roam this old earth after we trust Jesus as our Savior is to help others do the same. Those who hear our message are always skeptical at first because they only hear what we say. Their next step is to see if what we do lines up with what we say. And they don't want to watch us when we're having a good day. They want to know what happens when we get hit where we live. They want to see if we really believe what we say.

"You are what you do," some have said. But I think the opposite is true, as a movie I saw recently helped me to realize. "You do what you are." Your actions are a product of who you are.

The Shipman corollary to this is "You pop what you are." If I fill a balloon with my lungs and prick it with a pin, only my own hot air will escape. If you fill a balloon with water and throw it at me, only water will come out when it breaks over my head. When the pressure is on and you pop, what comes out of you in your actions is nothing more than a picture of what already lives inside of you. And people know this. So when they hear you say that Jesus is the way, they may only choose to believe you when they see how you respond when the world is against you. If you really walk with and trust in Jesus, it won't matter if the sun is shining or the rain is pouring. Your life will prove it in what you do.

> But even if you should suffer for righteousness, you
>   are blessed.
> "Do not fear what they fear or be disturbed,"
> but set apart the Messiah as Lord in your hearts,
>   and
> always be ready to give a defense to anyone
> who asks you a reason for the hope that is in you.
> *1 Peter 3:14–15a*

Those without Jesus do not have this kind of hope. They do not have a reason to hope when they hurt. So when they see that you do, they will be drawn to you like a magnet. Your ministry is to share your hope, even and especially during times of suffering. Always be prepared.

It's OK to tell others how you feel.

After this, when Jesus knew that everything was
now accomplished,
that the Scripture might be fulfilled,
He said, "I'm thirsty."

John 19:28

So far in our journey through the seven last words of Jesus on the cross, we find Jesus reaching out to others. Here at the midpoint, however, we find a startlingly human plea for help. The mouth that once spoke hydrogen and oxygen into existence now cries out for a drink of water. Jesus' loss of blood was so great by this time that his body begged for replenishing fluids. He openly shared this need with those around him, and they responded by offering him a drink.

Pain can sometimes drive us into seclusion. Rather than call attention to ourselves, we run away and hide. Of course we are rarely physically able to escape the crowd, so instead we lose ourselves in it and hide the pain that we feel. We deny our feelings with a smile, a nod, and a little white lie like "I'm doing just fine, thank you."

God never intends you to be alone during your trials. He wants and expects you to be in the company of others. That's why churches and families and friendships exist. When one person suffers, the others can help carry you along.

I am a member of several social groups in which I can confidentially share my struggles and ask for advice, prayer, and support. I am in a marriage where my wife hears complaints and fears that no one else does. Just a few minutes ago I called her to share my growing fear that I will not be able to complete this book on time. Her response was so comforting to me that I am now much more relaxed and able to write more freely to you.

I am a part of a men's integrity group. Once a week I sit down with one or more other guys and talk about my successes, failures, and struggles. We share the common struggles of being husbands and fathers and businessmen and handymen and servants of God all in the same day. When we sense that someone in the group isn't being completely honest or forthcoming in a particular struggle, we press him for more—not so we can pry but so we can promote healing.

I am a part of a home group, five to seven families from my church family who meet together weekly in one another's homes. We study the Bible a little, but we talk to one another a lot. If you walked in on us at any given moment, you would likely hear either a prayer request or a prayer. Our goal is to drop the facades that we tend to put on in front of others and really share what is going on in our lives. We challenge and encourage each other. And when one of us hurts, all of us share the burden.

This week in our inaugural home group meeting, I asked each person what he or she would miss most if he or she stopped attending church. Every single one said the same thing. They did not say "the music" or "Bible study" or "great sermons." They all said they would miss the fellowship, the friendship they had with one another.

I could not survive without the aid of these groups. And there are more that I haven't mentioned. My larger church family, friends who don't fall into any particular category, parents, siblings, and others—all play key roles in keeping me on track.

If you are like most folks, though, statistics indicate that you are largely disconnected from other people. You live in a sub-division or area where you know little or nothing about your neighbors. You drive long distances to get to work and have no real ties to your coworkers. You go to a church where you see people on Sunday whom you don't really know or see much the rest of the week. You are active in church programs, but you come and go without ever establishing real relationships. Your hobbies are things that you do alone or require traveling many miles to parti-cipate with strangers. You rarely have company in your home. If you have a dining room, you've converted it to something else because you don't have people over often enough to justify the big table. You never really share your deepest struggles with anyone other than your spouse, if you even have one and your relationship is good enough that you can really talk to each other.

We've come a long way from the village where everyone knows everyone else. Modern technology has given us the ability to sepa-rate where we live from where we do everything else. And in the process we have allowed ourselves to become isolated and detached from human contact. One of the few ways in recent history that technology has reversed this trend is on-line chat rooms. Millions of people are now searching cyberspace to find a sense of community and belonging because that is the only place they know to look.

You can reverse the trend, too, and not just on-line with people you may never see face-to-face. If these statistics define you as average, what I am about to suggest may seem radical. You need a village. You need a group of close Christian friends whom you can meet with weekly outside of the church building. If your church has home groups, then join one. If they don't, start your own. You don't have to have an immaculate plan, and it doesn't need to be "official." Just get together. Even if all you do is share a meal and some laughs, you will already have begun to break down social barriers, and that will bring you closer in the weeks to come. You will begin to share your goals, dreams, and struggles with one another. You will eventually reach a point where you can actually share your pain and ask for help. And you will get it.

Don't become a statistic. Don't be an island. Be a part of a village. Your pain will be much easier to bear when others help you carry it.

It's OK to tell God how you feel.

And at three Jesus cried out with a loud voice,
"Eloi, Eloi, lema sabachthani?"—which is
translated,
"My God, My God, why have You forsaken Me?"
Mark 15:34

God is perfect. You are not. So shape up, dress up, and hold your chin up. He's coming.

I used to feel that way. For a long time you could divide my Christian life into two parts, the real me and the Sunday me. The Sunday me really wasn't any different; I just had a candy-coated shell, and I sat in a pew near the front.

My disguise wasn't an attempt to hide rebellious sin. I had plenty of that, but I trusted God to forgive me when I confessed. What I was trying to hide from God and everyone else were doubt, confusion, and even disappointment with God. The messages I heard from the pulpit were typically so far removed from where I actually lived that I figured I must have been doing something really wrong. The others at my church seemed content to say, "God is in control." I told my mouth to say these words on Sunday, but sometimes I just couldn't do it the rest of the week.

During one dark episode of my life, I remember driving to the beach in the middle of the night. I was angry with God. Nothing in my life was going right. I stood on the shore where water meets sand. I cried. I yelled. I threw something, though I can't remember what. Years of suppressed emotions came tumbling out. All of my life I had tried to hide my disappointment with God from him because I thought he would be angry with me for feeling that way. I thought I had to get my act together before I came to God. But on this night I was meeting with God without my usual disguise, and he saw everything.

And do you know what God did when I finished? He held me. Oh, my feet were on the sand, but God was holding me. He did not condemn me for my feelings, and he did not tell me to shape up. He simply held me and told me that he would take care of everything.

At that stage of my life, I had never before experienced the God who would allow me to vent my feelings so freely. I even wondered if I was experiencing something psychological and not spiritual because how could a holy God listen to the kinds of things I had to say? I shouldn't be able to express doubts and fears to God. I have to be perfect, like Jesus.

Jesus was perfect, but even in his flawless life he never tried to hide his feelings of desperation. In the garden before his arrest, he begged three times for the crucifixion to be taken away from him. It wasn't, and he knew it wouldn't be because he came to the earth for that very reason. But still he asked. And during that prayer he was so overcome with dread at the thought of hanging on the cross and being separated from his Father that he sweat drops of blood. And then on the cross, as he experienced that separation firsthand, he cried out and asked, "Why, God, why? Why have you left me here to die?"

I've been told by many Christians never to ask why because there is always a reason and I should just believe that and keep walking. I know there is always a reason, but when I don't know the reason, I want to know *why.* So I ask. And now I am no longer afraid to ask why because Jesus did too.

God will take your dismay over your disguise any day. He does not want people dressing up for him. He wants his children to come to him honestly, whether in praise or in protest.

If you doubt what I'm saying, study Psalms. The largest book of the Bible is filled not only with commendations for God but also with complaints. Frequently David asked God why or when. He shared his complaints that God seemed to delay his answer to prayers or did not seem to care about his current situation. But always after David voiced his objections to God, he admitted that he had nowhere else to go and decided to wait on God for resolution.

Where else can you go when you are disappointed with God? Nowhere. So what do you do? You go to the source of your disappointment. You tell God how you feel. He wants to hear from you, and he will not condemn you. He will take you just as you are, but he will leave you new and improved.

It's OK to give up.

Jesus called out with a loud voice,
"Father, into Your hands I entrust My spirit."

Luke 23:46

Three times on this day Jesus gave up. He gave up to the authorities when they arrested him without cause in the garden. He gave up and fell down when the weight of the cross became too much for him to bear. And he gave up the fight for life altogether and trusted his Father to take him home.

Jesus' words are not just a dying request; they are Scripture. He was quoting Psalm 31:5. Reading the whole of Psalm 31, you will find that it is not a poem about death or surrender. It is a poem about survival and hope in the midst of great hardship. When Jesus gave up, he was not waving the white flag of surrender. He was giving up on his own human power in order to allow the strength of his Father to get him through circumstances he did not want to face alone.

Our human nature begs us and our independent culture trains us to fight the tendency toward dependency. We don't want to give up. We want to do everything in our own strength. We think we must fight to survive, not fall down. We try to depend only on ourselves, not on some invisible God.

Sometimes I deliberately challenge my son to try things I know he cannot do. I might ask him to pick up something heavy or touch something way beyond his reach or bring me something I know he cannot find. He will always try to complete these tasks himself at first, but inevitably he comes back to me. He grabs my hand and pulls me into the middle of his tough spot. Then he stops, looks up at me, and says, "Help, Daddy." This, of course, is exactly what I wanted in the first place.

I don't want my son to try and do everything on his own because I know he can't. And I purposely place him in these predicaments so that he will learn for himself that it's OK to give up and ask me to take over.

Our Father is the same way with us. He sometimes gives us impossible tasks and allows us to find ourselves in dilemmas with no apparent way out. He is not abandoning us. In fact, he is doing just the opposite. He is training us to depend on him.

When pain and suffering bring you to the edge of your wits and you do not know what else to do, stop trying. Give up. Lay your struggle at the feet of Jesus, and tell him plainly that you cannot deal with it anymore. Then wait for his answer. He will not let you down.

It won't last forever.

When Jesus had received the sour wine, He said, "It is finished!"
Then bowing His head, He yielded up His spirit.

John 19:30

Above Jesus' head on the cross was a small wooden sign. This was not unusual. In Jesus' day the authorities labeled criminals by their crimes. Those confined to prison would have their signs attached just outside the jail cell. If you and I could walk down a first-century prison corridor, we might see signs like "James of the Jordan: Stealer of Wheat" or "John of Joppa: Evader of Taxes" or maybe even "Barabbas of Bethany: Rebel of Rome."

In an execution the sign hung on the cross above the head. The two thieves on either side of Jesus probably had signs, too, but they did not capture the attention of even one of the Gospel writers. But all four took note of Jesus' sign and recorded its words for us. His sign read: "Jesus of Nazareth: King of the Jews."

When a criminal completed his prison sentence or died in an execution, the authorities took the sign and scrawled a single Greek word across it. That word best translates to English as "it is finished." It signified that the crime had been paid and no longer defined the person. The time of punishment was over. The person was free.

This is the same word that Jesus saved as his last, and it is packed with hope for you and me. When Jesus said, "It is finished," that single word had a thousand meanings. It signifies the successful completion of Jesus' mission on earth. It declares that we can be forgiven from sin because Jesus paid the price himself. And it also shows us that the painful trials we go through will not last forever. We will see an end to the pain.

Persistent pain brings tunnel vision, and we forget that what we are going through will not last forever. Most people who commit suicide fail to see an end to whatever plight drives them to such an unfortunate demise. The only way they can see to end their misery is to bring an end to life itself.

In early high school I seriously considered committing suicide. And do you know why? Because I had acne. My face had more pimples than a forest has trees. Someone I thought was a friend once called me Pizza Face. His assessment was accurate, but once I heard those words from one person, I became convinced that everyone else felt the same way about me. Every night I would cry out to God to make my face clear again. Every day I would wake up and look in the mirror and see that my condition was only getting worse. I saw no way to kill the acne short of killing its host.

My parents were sympathetic, though, and took me to a dermatologist. He prescribed a new drug and told me to take it three times a day. Later that year the acne completely disappeared, and I haven't had it since.

Do you know how long this epidermal epidemic endured? Less than one year. I almost gave up my life because I experienced difficulty for ten months. Looking back, I can even see a purpose for the pimples. They helped me be more sensitive to other people who are depressed and hurting. They made me realize that God does answer prayer, just not necessarily according to my schedule. And I also learned that God doesn't let me suffer through trials forever. He always brings me through my trials. And he will do the same for you.

Now the God of all grace,
who called you to His eternal glory in Christ Jesus,

will personally restore, establish, strengthen, and
support you
after you have suffered a little.

1 Peter 5:10

Don't let your current situation bring you so far down that you convince yourself you will never see the light of day again. God promises to give you relief but probably not according to your schedule and in the way that you imagine. But he will keep his promise to you.

How we react to pain is largely communicated in what we do, not what we say. When I get hurt, my tendency is to say and do things that I should not. I want to gripe, complain, thrash about, and otherwise do whatever is necessary to let everyone in the world know that I am not a happy camper.

Jesus could have preached a sermon on the meaning of his crucifixion, but his actions were enough. He could have decried the evils of capital punishment and called for the people passing by to riot. He could have called ten thousand angels to soar down from the heavens in attack formation and destroy his accusers and rescue him from his pain. He could have rallied his disciples into war with a stirring speech. He could have just griped the whole time.

We can learn much from the words that Jesus did not say. He did not curse or complain, a habit that so saturates our society that those who do not participate seem oddly out of place. But that's what Christians are, odd and out of place. We are only on this earth temporarily to bring the message of Jesus to others. And complaining serves our cause no purpose. We are called to a higher standard.

Do everything without grumbling and arguing, so
that you may be blameless and pure, children of God
who are faultless in a crooked and perverted generation,
among whom you shine like stars in the world.

Philippians 2:14–15

The absence of words can do just as much good as their appearance in most situations. As many good people before me have said, "If you can't find something good to say, don't say anything at all."

There. We've done it. We've filled our prescription and taken our medicine together. We've learned what Jesus did in the height of his own pain and discovered practical examples of how we can do the same. Now we can put down this book and embrace the heartaches.

It's not that simple. You know it. I know it. If you were hurting at the beginning of this chapter, you are probably still hurting. If you're not, don't hold your breath too long because your time is coming. I don't want you to leave this chapter thinking that all you have to do is follow a magical formula and everything will be OK. That's not how it works.

Here's how it works.

You will experience pain. You will not like it. God may choose to offer you complete freedom from your pain, and sometimes he may only choose to provide you with the grace to get through it. Until he comes, people will suffer and people will die, including you. Until he comes, the answer to pain does not lie in its absence; it lies in what you do with it.

For you were called to this,
because Christ also suffered for you,
leaving you an example,
so that you should follow in His steps.

1 Peter 2:21

Discussion Questions

Name the people who have hurt you recently. Have you forgiven them? Can you? Will you? When someone hurts you, do you retreat or fight back? How can you change your behavior during your anger in such a way that you are able to focus on others rather than yourself?

During an episode of pain, are you more or less likely to continue pointing the way to God to others? How can your pain actually draw others around you to Jesus?

Do you paint smiles over your pain or do you shout and let everyone know how bad you feel? What should you do in terms of sharing your pain when you hurt? What's the best approach for you?

One of the most difficult things of your Christian life may be being honest with God about how you feel. You don't have to cover up your feelings. God wants honesty. How do you feel about the pain you have experienced in your life? Have you shared these feelings with God? What's stopping you?

Do you try and carry on "business as usual" during your struggles? Have you ever really just collapsed before God and "given up"? Don't be afraid to try.

---

1. Alice Gray, comp., *More Stories from the Heart* (Sisters, Oreg.: Multnomah Publishers, 1997), 126–27.

Finding God in Unexpected Places

CHAPTER TWELVE

*A man's spirit is the highest part . . . the part which lasts when
the physical part . . . has vanished. It is the spirit of a man which
is the source and origin of his highest dreams and thoughts and
ideals and desires. The true, the genuine worship is when man,
through his spirit, attains to friendship and intimacy with God.
True and genuine worship is not to come to a certain place; it is
not to go through a certain ritual or liturgy; it is not even to bring
certain gifts. True worship is when the spirit, the immortal and
invisible part of man, speaks to and meets with God, who is
immortal and invisible.*

—WILLIAM BARCLAY

Where is God?

This question is asked as often as the sun rises. You've asked
it. I've asked it. Many times we seek the answer during times of
trouble. I've addressed many of those issues in previous chapters.
This time I ask the question of you—and in an entirely different
context.

When my son asks, "Where is Daddy?" he never means "Why
isn't Dad here now to bail me out of this tough spot?" In his world
this question mostly means "Is Daddy around because I want to
include him in what I am doing right now." He wants me to sit

down and play ball or cars or puzzles. He wants me to watch him jump and dance and march around the room. He wants me to help him get to things he can't and help him explore things he doesn't understand. He wants me to put him on my shoulders and tickle his tummy. He just wants me to be with him.

One of the names of Jesus in the Bible is *Emmanuel.* This name means "God with us." Jesus is God *with* us. He is not "God over us" or "God commanding us" or "God way out there watching us from a distance." He is God with us. He is right here, right now.

You cannot escape the presence of God any more than you can escape the beating of your own heart. He is there. Whispering. Waiting to be recognized. Splashing sunsets on the horizon. Bringing a bird-song wake-up call to your window. Peeking between the newspaper headlines to say, "I have better news for you." Longing to walk beside you during your day. He is everywhere, even in the most unexpected places. Even in a box of doughnuts.

Lois awoke on Sunday morning with a heavy heart. Her husband was ill. He had been in and out of the hospital for some time. His absence from work made the finances extra tight this month. They had already missed one car payment and were dangerously close to missing a second. Still, Lois tried to keep her hopes up as she dressed for church.

She stared into the mirror, making sure that everything was just right and praying quietly about her situation. As she talked with God, she suddenly remembered she was supposed to buy doughnuts for the continental breakfast served at the church each week. "Oh, God," she thought. "I can't afford doughnuts. We have no cash as it is. The bills are stacking high. You understand, right? I'm not going to buy doughnuts today."

God whispered back to Lois and told her to buy the doughnuts, that he would take care of her. Lois hesitated but thought,

No, Lord. I can't. I just can't. Back and forth she went in her prayers, but her final decision was to save the money. What difference would a little box of doughnuts make anyway?

Lois was already running late but decided to take the matter to her husband, hoping he would reassure her that she was right. He chuckled and said, "Lois, just buy the doughnuts. We can spare a few dollars, and you can spare a few minutes. Call the store, and they'll have them ready for you when you arrive."

Lois was outnumbered. Both God and her husband were against her. With a deep sigh she dialed the number and ordered the doughnuts. She picked them up and made it to church right on time.

As she set the doughnuts down, the pastor of the church walked over to her and greeted her warmly. "Lois," he began, "the elders and I are aware of what's going on in your family. I want you to know that we discussed and prayed about your situation, and the Lord led us to give you this."

Lois stared incredulously at the check in the pastor's hand. The amount was enough to cover two car payments and doughnuts for weeks to come. Lois hugged the pastor and took her seat as the worship service began. The songs and the sermon took on new meaning because God was with her and she knew it.

Lois never misses a Sunday if she can help it. And if you catch her between her car and the church building, you will see a Bible in one hand and a big box of doughnuts in the other.

God loves it when you worship him in church and seek him in the Bible and talk to him in your prayers, but he wants his relationship with you to continue in between those high points. You don't have to look far to find him. He may not be any further than your own backyard.

That's exactly where I found God tonight. I recently purchased a telescope. My intent that night was to inspect the moon. I did not plan on seeing God when I focused the mirrors and lenses on the lunar surface, but that is exactly what happened. Having only observed the moon with the naked eye before, I was taken aback by the clarity of detail. I saw beautiful plains, breathtaking mountains, deep valleys, and colossal craters. All I could think of was God. He made this moon and placed it in the sky. He arranged it so that the moon would appear in its various phases each month. He made it the perfect size and placed it at just the right distance to allow spectacular solar eclipses. He made it a work of art for us to enjoy and explore.

And that's just the moon. My meager forays into observing the planets and stars have had no less an effect on my awe of God and his creation. The grandeur of Saturn's rings, the moons of Jupiter, and the Great Orion Nebula have all sent shivers down my spine.

I guess I shouldn't be so surprised. After all, the Bible predicted my fascination with the night sky:

> *The heavens declare the glory of God;*
> *the skies proclaim the work of his hands.*
> *Day after day they pour forth speech;*
> *night after night they display knowledge.*
> *There is no speech or language*
> *where their voice is not heard.*
> *Their voice goes out into all the earth,*
> *their words to the ends of the world.*
>
> *Psalm 19:1–4*

God is present in creation. And he isn't just sitting idly by. He is talking—even shouting—trying to get our attention and say, "I am here, and I made all this for you."

Creation and pastries aren't the only places we can find God. There is no place on this planet where God is not. He is everywhere. You can even find him in the cemetery.

❧ ❧ ❧

<table>
<tr><td>Based on
Matthew 28:1–10;
Mark 16:1–11;
Luke 24:1–8</td><td>*After Jesus died on Friday, a group of women came to his tomb early Sunday morning. Their purpose was to embalm his body in spices and mourn his passing. They expected to find only death and disap-*</td></tr>
</table>

pointment. Instead, they found something entirely different.

On their way to the tomb, the women wondered aloud how they would get inside. They knew that its opening was sealed with a large stone that none of them were strong enough to move aside. They may or may not have known that a squadron of sixteen Roman soldiers stood outside with explicit orders to block the entrance until Sunday evening. Still, they followed the path through the olive grove toward the artificial cave where they last saw Jesus' body.

Their hearts were heavy as the sun's first rays scattered over the horizon. They had seen him die. They heard his final words. They watched a Roman soldier thrust a spear through his rib cage and into his heart. They saw his limp body fall as Joseph and Nicodemus took Jesus down from the cross and hastily wrapped him in grave clothes. They followed the men to the tomb and watched them place his body inside and seal up the entrance at sundown on Friday, just as the Sabbath day began. They resolved to return at first light on Sunday morning to give Jesus a more suitable burial.

And now they rounded the last bend in the path and approached the tomb. Their eyes were still adjusting to the growing light of morning. That's when they noticed that the large stone was missing from the tomb's entrance. The Roman soldiers were gone. Startled, they dropped their spices and ran through the dark opening and to the place where the body was. Was. Now only the grave clothes lay on the rocky resting place cut into the side of the wall. They looked at one another but did not speak. What could this mean? Where was Jesus?

Just then, two angels gleaming in white clothes appeared. The women fell to the ground in awe and fright. The angels spoke. "Don't be afraid. We know that you are looking for Jesus. But why would you come here to look for the living? This is a place reserved only for the dead. He is not here. He is alive! Don't be surprised by this news. He told you that he would die in this way, and he told you that he would live again after three days. Now go and tell his disciples the good news that he is alive."

The angels vanished as suddenly as they had appeared. The woman stood in bewilderment for some time before the sights and sounds of the past few moments began to crystallize. Then, as if by some unseen signal, they all began to run. They ran as fast as they could to tell the disciples what had happened.

Their emotions were on fire. Still frightened from the angel encounter in the tomb, they also felt pure joy at the thought that Jesus could really be alive. And just when they felt as if their lungs would not allow them to take another step, they halted in their tracks.

Jesus stood on the path in front of them. He spoke with a smile and stretched out his hands to greet them. Instantly they fell, clasping and kissing his feet. There they worshiped him. Some whispered quiet praises. Some wept. Some called his name over and over again. Some called him Emmanuel and shouted, "God is truly with us!"

I know what you're thinking. If only it were that easy. If only you could see God the way they did.

You can.

But how?

The women who saw Jesus first that morning have given us a few helpful hints.

Seek him now.

Early that Sunday morning Jesus' disciples remained locked in the room where they ate their last meal with Jesus. They were afraid that the sentence that Jesus faced might soon be their own. If Jesus could be so easily executed, then surely those who followed him would soon be tried, imprisoned, and perhaps put to death as accomplices. With no thought of where else to go or what else to do, they chose to stay in the place where their last good moment with Jesus still lingered in memory.

Meanwhile a group of women chose a different course of action. They awoke at first light, gathered burial spices, and headed toward the garden tomb. They went even though they had no idea how they would roll the stone away and get inside. They went even though Jesus lay dead. They went even though all they could do was delay the stench of death with perfumes. They sought God even when they thought he wasn't really there. They sought him the best way they knew how, and Jesus honored their efforts.

The disciples looked for God where they last saw him fully alive. The women looked for him in the spot where he seemed completely dead. Why did Jesus choose to reveal himself to the mourners in the cemetery before all others?

God wants you to experience his presence in every part of your life, including the places where you least expect to find him active. And while he loves to have you praise him at the height of your church's weekly worship service, he also longs for you to include him at every place in between.

In the days before Jesus visited the earth, when people wanted to find God, they went to the house of God, the temple, because that is where the presence of God hovered. Sometimes we forget that after Jesus came a dramatic relocation took place. When Jesus died, the giant curtain in the temple that separated the world from the place of God was torn in half. With an invisible sword God declared to us that we no longer have to go to the temple, or anywhere else, to experience him. The Spirit of God has been given to each of us, and now we cannot escape the company of God because he now lives in those of us who have volunteered to let him.

I repeatedly hear the church building today referred to as the house of God. This misnomer carries with it the misconception that we must be seated in pews in order to perceive the presence of God. Nothing could be further from the truth.

> *Do you not know that your body is a sanctuary of*
> *the Holy Spirit*
> *who is in you, whom you have from God?*
> *You are not your own.*
>
> 1 Corinthians 6:19

The body that now carries your soul and the weight of your daily concerns also carries with it the Spirit of God. He lives with you. He is there when you lie down to go to sleep and when you wake up in the morning. He is no stranger to the height of your workday when the unappreciative boss piles another endless stack of projects on your desk. God is with you in the crowded minivan as you taxi children all over town and try to get errands done before you have to reverse the route and pick them back up again. The Lord does not leave you when you face the most difficult struggles of your marriage. He is always there.

If this is really true, then why does God seem so absent in difficult situations? Why does it often appear that a large stone stands between us and Jesus? And even if we could get past it, we wonder if all we would find is a God powerless to help us right now.

It is because we aren't really looking for him. Instead of leaning on God and praying to him during these times, we shut him out because we feel that these tasks and trials are too worldly or even too unholy for his liking.

A fictitious rift in our culture attempts to divide secular from sacred. This invisible boundary did not always exist. It is a faulty product of the Enlightenment period, when humans began to value intellectualism over spiritualism. This prevailing philosophy's only contribution to our lives is the chilling license to confine God to the places that our brains deem most appropriate.

Fortunately for us, God neither sees nor confines himself to the limits of this boundary. He is always with us. He longs to be a part of every part of our day. So do not exclude him. Seek him. Go to the center of the location where he is most needed and look for him. Ask him to reveal himself to you in that place. Whether you stand at the tombstone of a lost loved one or at the base of an impossibly high mountain, look for him. He is there because he is in you.

Celebrate the past.

Preparing a body for burial is not just a routine aimed at slowing decomposition. It is a final, intimate moment intended to celebrate the life that once lived. The women who came to the tomb no doubt spent a good deal of time as they walked discussing the good times they had with Jesus. They expected to do the same inside the tomb as they anointed him with spices. Together they formed a makeshift funeral and collective eulogy.

The word *eulogy* means "good word." In a memorial service the eulogy brings to mind all of the favorable aspects of a person's life. Eulogies are most meaningful when we know the person and those good things touched our lives. The eulogy is meant to serve as a meaningful substitute for the presence of the missing person. Sometimes it is all we have.

When God seemed to be missing from the life of King David, he created a eulogy that we now call Psalm 77. In this short poem David grapples with God's absence in the present by remembering his presence in the past.

> *I cried out to God for help;*
> *I cried out to God to hear me.*
> *When I was in distress, I sought the Lord;*
> *at night I stretched out untiring hands*
> *and my soul refused to be comforted.*
> *I remembered you, O God, and I groaned;*
> *I mused, and my spirit grew faint.*
> *You kept my eyes from closing;*
> *I was too troubled to speak.*
> *I thought about the former days,*
> *the years of long ago;*
> *I remembered my songs in the night.*
> *My heart mused and my spirit inquired:*
> *"Will the Lord reject forever?*
> *Will he never show his favor again?*
> *Has his unfailing love vanished forever?*
> *Has his promise failed for all time?*
> *Has God forgotten to be merciful?*
> *Has he in anger withheld his compassion?"*
> *Then I thought, "To this I will appeal:*
> *the years of the right hand of the Most High."*

> *I will remember the deeds of the* LORD;
> *yes, I will remember your miracles of long ago.*
> *I will meditate on all your works*
> *and consider all your mighty deeds.*
>
> Psalm 77:1–12

Much of the purpose of the Bible is to help us remember what God has already done. It helps us become familiar with the character of God. It gives us the courage to believe that he will be consistent and do the same things again during our lifetime.

When God seems most distant to you, pull your Bible out and sit down. Spend some time reading how God consistently intervened in the lives of his people. And then remember that you are one of his people too. Then take the time to write down a few words of your own—a eulogy, if you will. How has God touched your life in the past? Cherish the moments when God revealed himself to you. Thank him for the ways he has touched your life.

Don't wait until Sunday. Do it now. Celebrate God's faithfulness wherever you are. In that celebration you will find the encouragement to wait until the time when he reveals himself again. Then you will have a new entry for your diary that you can recite during your next drought.

Hold on to the promises.

The Bible not only shows us what God has done in the past. It is full of God's promises for the present and the future.

Jesus assured his followers at least three times that he would be crucified and then rise again on the third day, but they never really understood what he meant. And with the vision of Jesus' death still fresh on their minds, these words faded from their memory.

No one, not even the women on the way to the tomb that morning, remembered Jesus' promises concerning his resurrection—not until the angels reminded them what Jesus said. Then everything seemed to come together.

God's promises can be easy to forget during a crisis, but they do not *change* during our crises. They stand for all time. In case your present situation has erased God's promises from your mind, let me remind you of just a few of them. If you have a Bible next to you, pull it out and look up the passages. If any of them seem particularly appropriate, or particularly hard to believe, those are the ones where you should spend the most time.

God will never leave you for any reason (Heb. 13:5).
God will always love you (Rom. 8:39–40).
If you trust Jesus, you will have eternal life (John 5:24).
If you seek God, you will find him (Prov. 8:17).
If you ask, God will forgive you (Isa. 43:25).
Every promise of God will be kept (Mark 13:31).
God will provide your every need (Phil. 4:19).
God will protect you from Satan and his schemes (2 Thess. 3:3).
God has a purpose for what is happening in your life
     (Rom. 8:28).
God will provide an escape for your greatest temptation
     (1 Cor. 10:13).
God will guide you in the decision you need to make
     (Prov. 3:5–6).

These promises are the heart of God. He will honor them all, along with a thousand others contained within the pages of your

Bible. They provide us with a confident hope that God is always with us and will always take care of us.

My little boy has a habit of wanting everything *now*. At bedtime he wants a sucker. An hour before I want to wake up in the morning, he wants breakfast. He begs to play when I am tucking him in for his nap. He wants to see his mother right after she walks out the door to run an errand.

Do you know what I do when Ryan asks for these things? I promise him he can have them, later. I don't just promise him because I want him to stop asking. I promise him to reassure him during the waiting period. Sometimes I even use promises to get him to obey me. "Ryan, if you will be quiet and lie down, when you wake up, you can have a sucker." As soon as he hears those words, it changes everything. He knows I mean business, so he lies down quietly and takes his nap.

God means business with his promises. His words have the power to change us because we know he means what he says. God's promises assure us during the waiting period between now and the time we meet him face-to-face in heaven that he is with us.

The last words Jesus spoke to his disciples before ascending into heaven were a promise. I can't help but think that these are the words he wanted us to remember most between that day and the day of his return.

> *And remember, I am with you always, to the end of the age.*
>
> *Matthew 28:20*

Discussion Questions

Have you ever asked, "God, where are you?" Have you ever found God in an unexpected place? Describe your experience(s).

Describe a moment when God seemed particularly far away. Now look back at that time and explain how God may have actually been right there in the middle of your struggle.

If you aren't feeling particularly close to God right now, review some of the times when you did feel very close to God. What were your experiences? Why did God seem so real?

What promises of God in the Bible are most important to you? How have you seen God's promises come true in your life?

Taking the Final Step

CHAPTER THIRTEEN

The Body of Benjamin Franklin,
Printer
(Like the cover of an old book
Its contents torn out
And stripped of its lettering and gilding),
Lies here, food for worms;
But the work shall not be lost,
For it will (and he believed) appear once more
In a new and more elegant edition
Revised and corrected
By the Author.

—EPITAPH OF BENJAMIN FRANKLIN

Writers are desperate readers. We'll read anything. No cereal box, billboard, or fortune cookie goes unread when I am around. Sometimes I will wander into a bookstore and read the first paragraph of every book on the shelf until time runs out. About the only thing I won't read is an instruction manual.

While writing this book I wandered over to my parents's house. They have been kind enough to lend me their travel trailer out back as a writing retreat. I was looking for something to read. I took the small-town newspaper and settled down to see what goes on in the piney woods of East Texas.

I read the story of eighty-three-year-old Janie Marie True. A former missionary and pastor's widow, she lived alone in a modest brick home in a small town not far from my parents. She still managed to get around town in her ten-year-old car to see her family and friends and to attend church as often as possible. She read her Bible every day. She was well respected in her community and spoke with her nearby nephew and his wife during the week.

On Friday morning Mrs. True drove by the bank on business and then returned home. At 11:30 A.M., the local Meals on Wheels brought her lunch. As with all visitors to her home, Mrs. True talked openly of her faith and provided two printed devotionals to the couple. The names of the devotionals were "The Value of Life" and "The History of Murder." Truly ironic considering what would happen next.

At around 1 P.M., a neighbor noticed her pick up her mail from the outside mailbox. Sometime shortly after 4 P.M., another neighbor noticed the garage door up and the car gone. Mrs. True would never have left the house with her garage door open.

Some time during that afternoon someone who knew Janie Marie came into her home, slit her throat, and stole her wallet. She died alone on the living room floor of her home as the perpetrator drove away in her car. Her body lay there until her nephew and his wife found her several hours later.

Her nephew, deeply saddened but not angry by the tragedy, commented that Janie Marie's last words were probably "God, forgive him."[1]

Janie Marie True did not deserve to die like that. But the newspaper story of her untimely death does not tell us what happened next. The last step we saw her take was in her living room, but she took one more step. She stepped out of her eighty-three-year-old body and into the presence of the God with whom she had walked and talked for so long. Though we are unhappy to see her go, Janie Marie wouldn't trade where she is now for anything.

Death is not the final step in life's journey. But what happens when we die? On this subject the Bible is clear. Those of us who have chosen to seek Jesus in this life will see him face-to-face in the next. And there we will stay forever.

The apostle John was about the same age as Janie Marie when he wrote the Book of Revelation. All of his fellow apostles

Based on
Revelation 1:12–18

were now gone. Each died a martyr's death and now lived in heaven. John was not yet a martyr, but his faith earned him a meager living in exile on the tiny island of Patmos in the Aegean Sea. Alone and perhaps forgotten by many, John spent his days in prayer, Bible study, and writing his friends on the mainland.

One of the things you miss most when you live in solitary confinement is the sound of another human's voice. John had not heard another human speak for some time, and he undoubtedly longed for companionship.

One Sunday there on the island, as John attended a church service with one person in attendance, he heard a voice behind him. It was a voice he had not heard in more than sixty years.

I turned to see the voice that was speaking to me.
When I turned I saw seven gold lampstands,
and among the lampstands was One like the Son of
   Man,
dressed in a long robe,
and with a gold sash wrapped around His chest.
His head and hair were white like wool—white as
   snow,
His eyes like fiery flame,
His feet like bronze fired in a furnace,

and His voice like the sound of cascading waters.
In His right hand He had seven stars;
from His mouth came a sharp two-edged sword;
    and
His face was shining like the sun at midday.
When I saw Him, I fell at His feet like a dead man.
He laid His right hand on me, and said,
"Don't be afraid! I am the First and the Last, and
    the Living One;
I was dead, but look—I am alive forever and ever,
and I hold the keys of death and Hades."

Revelation 1:12–18

When John fell down and stared at the feet of Jesus, he could not see the scars of death. He saw only the glowing fire of never-ending life. Jesus' feet were different. They had changed. They were now immortal.

The same thing will happen to you and me when we die. We will be changed. We will leave our decaying mortal bodies behind to claim immortal ones full of the fire of eternal life. We will never die. We will never cry. We will never face pain or failure or separation from God again.

You will get a new body.

Put the diet books away. Throw away the hair spray and the makeup. Leave the razor blades and nose-hair clippers in the drawer. Cosmetic surgery and liposuction cannot come close to improving your body the way God will when you enter into heaven.

John gives us a vivid description of Jesus' body from head to toe. What we see in Jesus is what we can expect to see in ourselves one day.

"His head and hair were white like wool." Though our basic appearance will still be recognizable to others, everything about the way we look will become perfect. The gray hair you dread taking over will one day become permanently radiant. Your face will be free of wrinkles, moles, acne, unwanted hair, and every other blemish. Your teeth will never require braces, fillings, caps, root canals, or substitutes.

Imagine what eternity will be like without the need or even the desire to look in the mirror or worry about what someone thinks about the way you look. Everyone, including you, will be a faultless work of art.

"His eyes like blazing fire." There will no longer be such a thing as age or disease. Your eyes will not need glasses or contacts or corrective surgery. If you are blind now, you won't be then as you marvel at the city God has created for you. If you cannot walk, get ready to do some dancing. Arthritis is through. Cancer canceled. Amputees will have ample time to amble along the streets of gold and shake hands with everyone they meet. The deaf will hear angelic choirs and the sweet voices of friends and God.

Your feet and knees and lower back will never ache again. Never again will you know the pain that comes from burns, cuts, scrapes, and bruises. No more broken bones. Dictionaries, if there are such things in heaven, will require new editions as all medical terms simply fade from their pages.

Your mind will no longer forget or become confused. The lines that today divide classes of intelligence will disappear. The Ph.D. will be indistinguishable from the G.E.D. Mental illness is forever banished. The formerly insane will deliver rousing speeches. The depressed will heave in moments of unbroken laughter. The autistic will relish new sensations of heaven.

Heaven permanently eliminates hospitals, doctors, patients, medicines, prosthetics, wheelchairs, inhalers, ambulances, walkers, and surgery. Our new bodies will not need them.

"His feet like bronze fired in a furnace." The nail scars on Jesus' feet are no longer visible. His pain is no more. The fiery trials that you now face on earth will serve only to burnish your soul into a living trophy for the halls of heaven.

You will never know the loss of a loved one. You will never have to plan or attend a funeral. Your eyes will never know tears. At no time will you know the pangs of disappointment. The burdens and baggage that you carry in this life will be checked at pearly gates when you walk through, and you won't be calling anyone to find out why they never made it to your mansion.

When I was a toddler, my parents tell me that I was navigating my way around a coffee table and fell. My mouth caught the edge of the table on my way down, popping loose the only two teeth I had so far. I screamed and cried and bled. And though I have no doubt this actually happened to me, I do not remember it. My earliest memory is my third birthday. I do not remember anything before that. I do not remember my shocking relocation at birth or all of the times I cried in the night for my mother.

Heaven will be like that. We will not remember the early days of our eternity, the childhood we had back on earth. Our earliest memories will be of heaven (see Isaiah 65:17–18). I'm sure we will hear about the "old redemption story." We will know that we came from an imperfect place. And we will know that we are in heaven only because of Jesus.

"His voice like the sound of cascading waters." Abilities that you never had before will suddenly be yours. I love music, but you don't want to hear me try to sing—yet. In heaven, stop by my place. You'll like what you hear. I will be writing and singing songs all day.

We will fly like the angels. We will dance without rehearsing. We will run faster than any Olympic gold-medallist ever has. We will never falter for the right words to say. We will frolic with lions, tigers, bears, and alligators. We will no longer fear heights and closed places and crowds.

We will never grow tired. Our breath will never fail us, and our muscles will never ache. Our bodies will be fueled by the strength of God forever and ever.

"His face was shining like the sun at midday." You will experience eternal happiness, peace, joy, and contentment. Heaven is not just about eliminating the negative; it is also about filling your life with indescribable good.

Think about the happiest moments of your life. Mine include my wedding day and the night my son was born. What about yours? Now try and imagine what it will be like to have those feelings of joy not just for one day or one moment but for all of eternity.

How much of our lives on this earth are spent wanting and pursuing something that we think we must have to be happy? In heaven, you will neither want nor pursue. You will have everything you want. Everything you need will be available to you at all times. You will finally know the true meaning of peace and contentment.

Our new bodies will never grow old. They will never die. They will be perfect forever.

You will see Jesus.

Though heaven is filled with golden boulevards and people we love, these are not what make heaven what it is. Heaven is not about the things we will enjoy. It is about the one who put those things there for us to enjoy. The first thing John ever noticed about heaven was Jesus.

Jesus made heaven. Jesus is heaven.

> *In my Father's house are many dwelling places; if not, I would have told you. I am going away to prepare a place for you. If I go away and prepare a place for you, I will come back and receive you to Myself, so that where I am you may be also.*
>
> *John 14:2–3*

All Jesus wants when we get to heaven is to be with us. All we should want when we get to heaven is to be with him.

When I come home from work in the evening, I have a hot meal waiting for me. My closets and drawers are probably restocked with clean clothes. My son is well groomed and well dressed. But I do not come for these things. I come home to be with my wife. She is the reason I want to come home at all.

Sometimes we forget that both this life and the next life are about Jesus. We fall into the trap that so many others do. We think that Christianity is a list of rules and requirements that help us earn our way to heaven. We get into the rut of being good, and we spin our wheels trying to earn the right to live in a perfect world after we die.

If you have slipped into that rut, take my hand and let me help you out. Christianity is not a religion; it is a relationship with Jesus. The Bible is not a list of rules. It is a love letter written to win over your affections. Jesus has asked you to marry him. When you say yes, the engagement begins. The wedding ceremony will take place in heaven at the end of time to seal the relationship forever.

Jesus loves you. That's Christianity. You love Jesus. That's heaven.

Your eternity has already started.

You will not start living forever on the day you enter heaven. You started living forever the moment you asked Jesus to enter your life.

In the fledgling beginnings of our forever life with God, he has given us brief glimpses into heaven through the Bible. But why? For what purpose has God teased us with a sample tasting of what we cannot yet experience? It is so we will live like citizens of heaven in the days before we arrive.

> *Since all these things are to be destroyed in this way, it is clear what sort of people you should be in holy conduct and godliness as you wait for and earnestly desire the coming of the day of God, because of which the heavens will be on fire and be dissolved, and the elements will melt with the heat. But based on His promise, we wait for new heavens and a new earth, where righteousness will dwell.*
>
> *Therefore, dear friends, while you wait for these things, make every effort to be found in peace without spot or blemish before Him.*
>
> *2 Peter 3:11–14*

Look around. Everything you see will be destroyed. Burned. Removed from existence. If we really know this to be true, then why do we spend so much time collecting and depending on the things we cannot take with us? Our mission, according to Peter, is to prepare ourselves to meet Jesus.

When John saw Jesus, he only noticed two things that were familiar to him on earth. The church (represented by the lampstands) and the Bible (represented by the sword coming out of Jesus' mouth). The only two things on this planet that will survive in the next world are the Word of God and the people of God. Everything else is dust.

This implies a clear directive. The people of God should tell the story of God's Word to reach more people for God. Everything we do should have this eternal purpose in mind. If you already know you are headed there, then invite everyone you know to come along.

Janie Marie did just that. Only God knows how many people will walk through the pearly gates because of her, or because of you.

What will the newspapers say about you when you are gone? What will Jesus say to you when you arrive? The answer to both questions is up to you.

I met a Christian woman today who jumped out of an airplane. She has a video to prove it. I marveled at her bravery. She responded, "It's amazing what you can do when you don't fear death."

I agree.

I don't have to fear death any more. Neither do you.

So what are we waiting for? We may not jump out of an airplane, but at least we can jump out of our comfort zones and start living our eternity today.

See you on the other side.

Discussion Questions

What are your greatest imaginations about heaven? What and whom do you think you will see? Who would you want to see first? What kinds of questions would you have for God?

What about your body? Do you hope to be different once you get to heaven?

Jesus . . . he is heaven. Do you feel that your relationship with him is so close that if you met him in heaven today you wouldn't really notice the change? What do you think you will do when you see Jesus face-to-face for the first time?

Are you living in fear of your own mortality? Are you short-changing God on your eternity? How can you live differently today knowing that you will see Jesus face-to-face soon?

---

1. John Sparks, *The Holly Lake Spectator*, a weekly section of the *Big Sandy and Hawkins Journal*, 30 January 2002, 1B–2B.